MW00344530

Survival by faith

A STORY OF FAITH, OBEDIENCE, AND REVELATION

Shawn-Ta Sterns Wilson

Survival by faith

A STORY OF FAITH, OBEDIENCE, AND REVELATION

Shawn-Ta Sterns Wilson

©2016 Shawn-Ta Sterns Wilson. All rights reserved.

All rights reserved. No part of this book may be reproduced by any mechanical, photographic, or electronic process, or in the form of a phonographic recording; nor may it be stored in a retrieval system, transmitted, or otherwise be copied for public or private use-other than for "fair use" as brief quotations embodied in articles and reviews-without prior written permission of the publishers Shawn-Ta Sterns Wilson.

The author of this book does not dispense medical advice. The intent of the author is only to offer information of a general nature to help you in your journey for a better more fulfilling life. In the event you use any of the information in this book for yourself, which is your constitutional right, the author and the publisher assume no responsibility.

Scriptures noted are taken from:
King James Version Bible
New King James Version Bible
New International Version

Limit of Liability/Disclaimer of Warranty: the author and publisher make no representations or warranties with respect to the accuracy or completeness of the contents of this work with specific disclaimer of all warranties, including without limitation warranties of fitness for a particular purpose. The publisher is not engaged in rendering legal, accounting, medical, or other professional services. If professional assistance or advice is sought, it would be necessary to hire the appropriate professionals for such advice. Neither the publisher nor the author shall be liable for damages arising therefrom. Any links to outside websites or organizations does not mean that the author or the publisher endorses the information that these sites or organizations provide or recommend.

Dedication

To my parents, Robert and Valerie Sterns.

Thank you for your love, support and encouragement.

Table of Contents

CHAPTER 1

Good Gifts

Many years ago I dated someone who was of a different religion. He was a wonderful man and treated me like a queen, but I knew our religious differences would be a challenge. After a few short months, I felt the Lord guiding me away from him. *"Can two walk together, except they agree?" (Amos 3:3)* kept coming to me, over and over again. Even though I knew I had to break it off with him, it wasn't easy to do. He was a great guy; mature, responsible, funny, supportive, encouraging, financially stable, an excellent father, and he knew how to treat a lady. He even opened doors for me, consistently. He got along well with my friends and family which is always a bonus. Was the Lord really telling me to walk away from him? Wasn't he the type of man that we women are supposed to wish for and hope to find? No matter how hard it was, I broke up with him out of spiritual obedience. It surely didn't make sense in the natural, but in my spirit I knew what I was being told to do.

Shortly after our breakup, he invited me out to dinner. I didn't want to give the impression we would get back together, so I was hesitant to accept the invitation. It seemed important to him, so I allowed the people-pleasing side of my personality to kick in and I said yes.

He was a great communicator. We both loved eating out and the extra incentive was going to a very popular, upscale restaurant I had never been to. I knew I should not re-open the door the Lord told me to close, but I buckled and went. After all, it was just dinner...right?

On the way to the restaurant we were in a car accident. The impact sounded horrible and felt terrible. I couldn't believe what had just happened. In a matter of seconds we went from laughing and being excited about our pending dining experience, to being terrified. The sound of the other car hitting ours was incredibly loud. When we came to a stop, I remember thinking how crunched up it must be after a collision like that. To this day, I'm amazed that the damages were so minimal. After working through insurance matters with the other driver and the police, we were still able to drive the car to the restaurant. On the way there, I remember looking out the window, whispering, "Okay Lord, I hear you loud and clear now." With every fiber of my being, I believe the accident was the Lord's way of telling me one last time to end the relationship. If what had just occurred was a warning from Him, I was not willing to take any more chances. What would the next warning message be if I chose not to listen? I certainly didn't want to find out. To paraphrase, *I Samuel 15:22, obedience is better than sacrifice.*

Being a true gentleman, he understood when I ended the relationship for good. He was disappointed, but he respected my decision. We are still friends and I appreciate him as such. For some reason, it was not meant for us to be anything more than friends.

Had I been obedient to the nudging of the Holy Spirit from the beginning, both of us would have been spared the frightening experience of the accident. I am thankful, although I initially turned my back on what my Heavenly Father guided me to do, He spared our lives that day. The Holy Spirit leads and guides, but the choice is always ours to make. We can ignore Him if we'd like but the consequences of spiritual disobedience can be great.

The good news is the rewards of spiritual obedience can be even greater. Let me share another story with you. As I sat in church one Sunday afternoon, I noticed the woman next to me. Literally speaking, she was reading her Bible just inches from her face. It shocked me.

I had never seen anyone do that before. As we age, we all joke about our eyesight failing but I had never seen anything to this extent, and it was nothing to joke about. She appeared to be a bit older than me, but she certainly was not elderly.

As best as I could, I tried to stay focused on the sermon but that was becoming increasingly difficult to do. During service, the Lord and I were having a conversation of our own. Sitting right there in church, just a couple rows from the pulpit, the Lord spoke to me, "Buy her a pair of glasses". I looked over at the lady, "Lord, I don't even know her." He didn't waiver and He didn't change one word.

I heard Him tell me again to buy her a pair of glasses. This went on for several minutes, back and forth. It was more me that was back and forth because His words remained the same. No matter what response I gave back to Him, He said the same thing over and over again, "Buy her a pair of glasses".

I figured this was a test. I had promised to be more obedient to Him. Christmas just passed and I invited friends and family to my home for dinner. After dinner, we sat around the table talking. I asked this question, "What gift would you give Jesus for his birthday if you could?" One by one, they all answered and when it became my turn to state my gift, I said, "Obedience to His will". Whatever He wanted me to do with my life, I vowed to submit to it that Christmas day. A couple weeks later, this encounter at church happened.

I left church that day wondering how in the world I would approach this woman whom I did not know. How would I ask her if she wanted me to buy her a pair of glasses? The first thing I thought to do was consult with our Bishop's wife. I told her what God put in my spirit but was concerned the woman may be insulted. She assured me that the woman would not be insulted but grateful. The next Sunday at church, I saw her in the lobby, right before service started. I asked if we could speak off to the side, so others could not hear our conversation. I must admit, I felt a little intimidated and uncomfortable but I knew this was what I was supposed to do. Just as the First Lady said, she was grateful that I would make such an offer. We set a date for me to pick her up and take her to get an eye exam and glasses. Before we parted ways that morning, she pulled out a small piece of paper. She wrote her name, phone number, and a short note, "God Bless You" and referenced a scripture; *James 1:17.* Off the top of my head at that time I could not recall that verse but I later looked it up. It read: *"Every good gift and every perfect gift is from above, and cometh down from the Father of lights, with whom is no variableness, neither shadow of turning."* I presumed the glasses were the gift she felt she was receiving, and it comforted me that she viewed our interaction as good.

As scheduled, I picked her up for the appointment a few days later. When we arrived at the vision center, they performed the exam.

The doctor said her vision was so bad that specialty glasses would need to be ordered and would cost several hundred dollars. None of this was good news to me. I wanted her to be able to go home that day with glasses so that she could read. Because this was right after Christmas, I also wasn't financially prepared to pay the cost they quoted for the specialty glasses.

Standing there in the vision center, I had another silent conversation with the Lord. "Are you sure this is what you want me to do: you know I don't have that much extra money right now?" Again, His words did not deviate from what He had initially told me in church. God bless this wonderful lady. I think even she was surprised at the cost. She leaned in toward me and whispered, "You don't have to purchase the glasses; they're too expensive." I thanked her for the consideration and let her know we would be ordering the glasses! We proceeded to the register where I paid the non- refundable deposit required to place the order.

In the car as I took her home she shared a personal story with me. She told me that she had been going through a lot of things recently and wondered if she still belonged to God. She let me know that she had even prayed and asked that He would show her a sign that she still belonged to Him. She said, I was that sign. "Here you are, a stranger, doing something like this for me" she said. We attended the same church but had never actually met before.

I'm sure at some point we probably greeted each other with a "good morning" or "have a blessed day" but we did not actually know one another. This made it hard for her to understand why I was helping her.

What He used me for meant the world to her and I could feel it in her words and tone of voice. Looking back to the day she wrote the note, I now believe the 'gift' she felt she was receiving was the confirmation she had been longing for from God. As she sat in the passenger seat telling me of her recent struggles, I was so grateful that God used me to give her the assurance she needed. I counted it a blessing to have been able to be a part of that experience with her. It would take a week for the glasses to come in.

During that week, I was out of town for a work-related conference. When I returned from my trip, I called to see what day she would be available to go get her glasses. I was excited for her to get them, and the last time we spoke right before I left, she was excited too. We both imagined how nice it was going to be that she would soon be able to sit in church with her Bible on her lap like most other people and be able to read it clearly. Surely, the next time we saw each other in church, we would speak and it would be more than a standard greeting. We considered ourselves friends now, divinely connected.

Her sister answered the phone when I called and what she said left me speechless. My new friend had passed away while I was out of town. My mind was overloaded. I had no idea she was that sick. She told me she had been going through some things, but never indicated that her health was so serious. I was very sad that she was now gone. She was funny, friendly, and quite easy to talk with. Although I had not known her long, I considered her passing a loss. I had lost out on the opportunity to get to know her even better. Regardless of the sadness I was feeling I realized something, which to this day helps me to remain obedient despite the cost. Had I not done as the Lord asked that day in church, this kind woman may have passed away without receiving confirmation that she truly belonged to Christ. I believe because of my obedience that day in church, she went to Heaven with peace in her heart.

A few days later I stopped by the vision center to let them know she had passed away. I owed a final payment for the glasses and wanted to see if I still needed to pay it. Since the glasses had been made specifically for her, the vision center would not be able to resell them. When I explained the situation to the sales associate, not only did I not have to pay the balance, they returned the non-refundable deposit. The Lord has proven time and time again that if I stay on course with what He asks of me, He will eventually reveal His reasons. Sometimes the revelations are immediate and sometimes they come later down the road. In the vision center that day, at the very moment the refund was made, I saw the big picture of all that

God had orchestrated in the entire situation:

- I vowed to be more obedient to Him.
- He gave me an opportunity to prove I was sincere in the vow I had made.
- She needed a sign that she still belonged to Him.
- He gave me another opportunity to prove my sincerity with my money. I knew I didn't have the money to spare and so did He. He never intended for me to do without.
- He returned the money because of my obedience.

There are no words to tell you what an amazing experience all of that was. I came to realize He wanted me to know that if I would just trust Him (have faith), everything would work out fine. Even though all of this happened many moons ago, I still feel a praise rise up on the inside that has to come out when I retell this story. To be used by God to be a blessing to someone else in a situation as serious as this was humbling. He could have chosen anyone to deliver the confirmation she needed, but He chose me. Not because I'm special, but because I opened my heart to be obedient to His will. I can guarantee if you leave yourself open, He will use you too. It truly was a privilege.

CHAPTER

2 New Year

The New Year, January 2013, rolled around and I claimed it was going to be the absolute best year of my life! That is not unusual though, most people make such proclamations whenever the New Year rolls around. Usually, they are more in the form of resolutions and become a topic of discussion for weeks thereafter. I gave up on making resolutions many years ago. Like many people, I could never stick to one. My intentions were always good, but I lacked in the follow-through.

The dictionary defines proclamation as a public or official announcement, especially one dealing with matters of great importance. When I made my proclamation, that's exactly what I did. I announced to myself and the world that 2013 would be my best year yet! As far as I was concerned, it was a matter of great importance. For some reason, I felt a stronger than usual need to declare that at the on-set of this particular New Year.

The proclamation was general, yet all encompassing. Resolutions tend to be a bit more specific. Some may say their New Year's resolution is to lose weight, save money, work harder for a promotion, eat healthier, etc. For me, I did not have one specific thing in mind that I would do differently or try to achieve. All I knew was that I wanted 2013 to be the best year of my life. I set no specifics on how I would accomplish that though. Maybe, in the back of my mind, I thought it would mean things like spending more quality time with my family, maximizing every good opportunity presented to me, and finding the good in all things. In hindsight, I believe what I was really looking for was a new perspective on life.

The reality of the New Year is that it started out a little rocky. The second week of January I had the worst headache. Sadly, for me to have a headache wasn't that strange. It seems I've lived my entire life with them for one reason or another. I've gone through periods in life where they seemingly disappear for long stretches of time, but they always find a way back. This particular one made its presence known, for sure!

There was a conference for my job I was scheduled to attend in a few short days. I remember praying that the headache would go away because if it didn't, I knew I would not be able to go. This headache was unlike any I could recall having—ever. Considering I've had headaches all my life, that's a pretty strong statement. One particular night, prior to the conference, I woke up from what had been a fairly peaceful sleep. As soon as I awakened, I realized tears began welling in my eyes and I couldn't open them.

I was afraid to lift my head off the pillow. Something wasn't right and I was afraid to move. The pain, from what felt like pressure, was intense. My head hurt so badly and it truly felt as if my eyes were going to pop out of my head. Despite having a long-standing history of headaches, none of this was normal or familiar to me.

As I lay there with my eyes closed, I prayed: "Lord, you know this is more than I can bear. Your word says that *"by your stripes we are healed." (Isaiah 53:5)* I touched my eyelids as softly as I could and continued my prayer. The next thing I remember saying was *"Physician heal thyself" (Luke 4:23)*. Honestly, I wasn't even sure if I was quoting the scripture in proper context to the situation. What I did know was that I was afraid and in pain. Because of that I was drawing on any and everything I could think of at that time and praying sincerely that the Lord would help me. If He didn't, I wasn't sure what I would do. I couldn't open my eyes so I was leery to get up. I had no idea what time it was but knew it was the middle of the night.

There is no other way to say this but to just say it. Within seconds of the prayers I uttered, the pain was gone. I don't make claims for the purpose of sensationalism. What I am saying is true and real. In a matter seconds, with the simple act of laying hands on my own eyelids, praying, believing, and drawing hope as well as comfort from scriptures, the pain was completely gone. Please understand, I am just your average, truly ordinary, person. I have no degrees in divinity or theology. I have never claimed to have healing power. As a matter of fact, I can't even confess that my faith has always been rock solid. Yet, because I believed in that very moment that it was possible for me to be healed and I turned to the Lord for help, I was healed! *"...according to your faith be it unto you" (Matt 9:29).*

Even though I believed it was possible to be delivered from the pain, and I certainly received my healing instantaneously, it caught me by surprise. No such thing had ever happened in my life before.

I was relieved to be free from the pain, but quite honestly, my first reaction was, "Oh my goodness, He did it! He heard the prayers that came straight from my heart and he took the pain away!"

I was in awe of what had occurred. Laying there in the same exact position, having never moved an inch, with my eyes still closed, I began poking at my eyelids. It seemed I needed to "test" this out. Had I truly been healed that quickly? Heaven knows I didn't want to doubt the Lord. Yet, I found myself dissecting and analyzing every aspect of what had just taken place to see if there was a 'logical' explanation. Isn't it funny how often we say things like, "God is able", but when He does something for us, we have a hard time believing He did it?

When I couldn't come up with a logical explanation, I decided to accept it for what it was, a blessing. A blessing of that magnitude surely deserved praise. Still laying in the same position, I began to praise God, right there! I didn't have to get up, get dressed, or do anything formal. I praised Him right where I was, right in the very spot where I received my healing. Afterwards, I was able to go back to sleep and slept comfortably the rest of the night.

I went to work the next day anxious to share my testimony. There are a few believers in the office who I knew would share in my excitement over what happened. However, the workplace isn't necessarily filled with those who welcome such conversations. We have been trained that discussions of this nature are inappropriate in the workplace. Yet there are some things that must be shared regardless. The miracle working power of God is one of them. Even if I wanted to keep it to myself, the word is pretty clear that I am not supposed to: *"But whosoever shall deny me before men, him will I also deny before my Father which is in heaven."(Matthew*

10:33) I've learned to share my testimonies freely because we can all benefit from them. Hearing a testimony reinforces for believers that 'God can' and 'God will'. For a non-believer, I pray it shows that God is alive and well and desires to operate in their life. Hearing testimonies of His miracle working power may draw them to Christ.

As I went through my day, I told my story from the night before to anyone who I thought might listen. Every time I retold it, I had a spirit of praise well up inside, all over again! When God does something for me, it's hard for me not to be grateful. It's hard to not praise Him.

Because of how He blessed me, I was able to attend the conference and reconnect with colleagues I had not seen in quite some time. I had even been asked to speak at a session which was the highlight of the conference experience. Public speaking is something that took a lot of getting used to, and I still can't say that I enjoy it. However, when I had the chance to speak with a room full of college students who were considering my career field as their profession, I realized that it wasn't public speaking for me. I was simply sharing my passion!

When I returned from the conference, I thought about how I would have missed out on this wonderful, professional event had I not exercised my faith. I could have laid there and cried or gotten up and taken medicine with the hope it would provide relief. Instead, I turned to God and sincerely relied on Him to help me, and He did.

CHAPTER

3 | *Unimaginable Pain*

The third week of January, I remember having nagging pain in my left shoulder from what I assumed was a strained muscle. I had felt it for a couple of days since returning from a conference in Orlando. When I came home, I remember picking my suitcase up off the bedroom floor and slinging it on top of my bed to unpack.

A pulled muscle seemed a reasonable likelihood because of the awkward movement and weight of the suitcase. As such, I thought I would be fine in a few days, once the muscle healed.

I talked with a co-worker about the muscle strain and he suggested I take two over-the-counter pain pills. He had some in his office and

I agreed to take them. Within an hour, I felt much better, which made me feel pretty silly for walking around in pain when two small pills were all I apparently needed! For the next few days, life went on as normal and what I presumed to have been muscle pain did not bother me again.

On the night of January 21st, one of my Chihuahuas (Dottie) was having an extremely difficult time breathing. Her breathing was labored and all she could do was lay on her side. She wouldn't move. She wouldn't eat or drink. This was in the middle of the night so all I could do was make her as comfortable as possible, and pray that she didn't die. If she could get through the night, I would take her to the vet in the morning. Strangely enough, when morning came she seemed to be doing better, but I decided she still needed to be seen by a vet. What I saw the night before worried me and I wanted an explanation for what had been bothering her. I went to work and called their office as soon as they opened and was given an afternoon appointment. I contemplated whether or not I should stay home with her until the appointment, but she did seem to be doing okay. She was up walking around, and I saw her drink a little water so I went on to work.

As best as I could, I tried to get through my work day. I was still concerned about Dottie and felt guilty for leaving her home by herself when I knew she didn't feel one hundred percent. I prayed that I would not get home and find that she was gravely ill again or had passed away. By mid-morning, while sitting at my desk working, I realized I was becoming more and more uncomfortable. It wasn't about Dottie though. It seemed that the pain in my left shoulder was coming back. "No worries, I'll take care of this", I thought. I went to my co-worker's office to see if he had any more of the over-the-counter pain pills he had given me earlier in the week. Based on my last experience after taking them, I knew that it would only be a matter of an hour or so before I would be feeling better again.

He did have more, so I took two and went back to my office. This time, the pills did not have the same immediate effect as they did before. In fact, as the minutes passed by, I felt worse and worse. The pain seemed to radiate from the front, left of my upper chest all the way through to my shoulder blade in the back. I didn't think I was having a heart attack because I wasn't clammy or sweating. The location of the pain made me wonder however. I was becoming concerned enough that I called for the paramedic. This was not a 911 call. Where I work, we often have paramedics on duty to cover event activity. Sadly, calling a paramedic while at work was not a new thing for me. Because of my food allergies, I've called upon them before when I've accidentally eaten something that I should not have.

I told the paramedic all of my symptoms. He hooked me up to an EKG machine to read my heart rhythm. Everything checked out fine.

That was the good news. The bad news was that I was still feeling terrible and didn't know why and neither did he. He suggested that I go to the ER. By this time it was getting close to Dottie's appointment, and all I could think about was getting her to the vet so she could be seen. That was my priority at the moment. Probably not the best decision I could have made, but I was concerned about her.

I left work to go home and get her. While driving, the discomfort worsened. I couldn't find the right position to sit in the driver's seat so I squirmed around the entire drive home. Dottie was my main focus, so I pushed through the pain and discomfort. When I got home, it was as if I were on a military re-con mission (get in and get out). I quickly picked her up, got back in the car, and headed back downtown to the vet's office. Dottie seemed fine and was enjoying the ride, but there was nothing enjoyable about it for me. Having the seatbelt draped across my left shoulder was beyond uncomfortable and painful. Holding the steering wheel with my left hand was becoming impossible. Sitting in a normal, upright position in the driver's seat was more than a challenge. By the time I arrived at the clinic, I had moved from being in extreme discomfort to being in all out agony.

I cried the entire time I was in the lobby of the clinic waiting for Dottie to be seen. The staff in the office tried to comfort me as they thought I was crying because of Dottie. I didn't have the heart to tell them I wasn't. As a matter of fact, I really couldn't say much of anything, nor could I sit for long. Sitting became tough, so I stood. After a few minutes I couldn't stand, so I sat. In between, and all through, I cried. I was miserable! I had no idea what was wrong but knew as soon as Dottie got taken care of, I was going to the hospital. It amazes me what we pet parents will do for our furry, four-legged friends.

After being examined by the vet, it was determined that Dottie's discomfort the evening before was caused by a fairly minor digestive problem. I was astonished that something so minor could have caused her to exhibit such drastic symptoms, but I was thankful it wasn't anything more serious. Above and beyond being thankful, I was eager to leave. I needed medical attention myself!

When we left the clinic, suffice it to say, it was all I could do to get home safely. In hindsight, there is no way I should have been behind the wheel of a car. The thought of having an ambulance come get me from the vet did cross my mind. Why didn't I do that? Dottie. I didn't want her to have to stay at the vet until I could find a way for someone to get her. Isn't that just like a mother? It didn't matter that it was a dog I was putting before me, mothers by nature typically put everyone and everything before themselves!

On the way, I called my son and asked that he meet me at home… ASAP. I explained that I had no idea what was wrong and I was in severe pain and needed to go the emergency room. The pain became more intense and seemed to be coming in waves. It hurt constantly and there were moments when it would intensify, then subside, intensify again, and subside again. This was the craziest thing I had ever experienced.

Thankfully, even with the modest rush hour traffic, the vet's office was only a 20-minute drive from my house so I didn't have to be in the car too long. Dottie and I made it back to the house safely which was a blessing in itself. How I saw the road through tear-filled eyes is beyond me. How I drove with her on my lap, my left shoulder, arm, and hand useless, steering the wheel with my right hand only, sitting sideways in the seat, and all at the same time managed to make a telephone call for help, and arrive home safely was the grace of God alone! At that moment, I was the poster child for everything you should not do while driving.

Have you ever heard someone say that truth is stranger than fiction? Well, it really is an accurate statement. I cannot explain this, but by the time I got home the pain was gone. Just gone! It had vanished as if it had never been there to begin with. When my son arrived at the house, I was extremely worn out. I had not slept well the night before because Dottie had been in distress. On top of that, I had just spent a couple hours crying from physical pain. The drive home was frightening, unbearable, and stressful. All I wanted to do was sit in my recliner for a while to regain some strength and decompress. I still wanted to go to the hospital, but I just needed to rest for a short while. That "short while" turned into about five hours. For five solid hours there was no pain, so I chalked it up as a fluke. I told my son that I was fine and no longer wanted or needed to go to the hospital. He left and I went to bed, cased closed, but mystery unsolved. It didn't matter to me anymore what had been wrong. I was just happy that whatever it was, was gone. January 22nd had been a memorable day for sure. All I wanted to do was put it behind me and, for a couple of hours, I was successful.

Sometime around 11 pm, I woke up with pain that words will never be able to describe. I am three years removed from that experience now, yet still have not found a suitable way to explain what I felt. I simply recall waking up in excruciating pain. The pain was in the left side of my chest, through my body to my left shoulder blade, and all the way down my left arm to the tip of my index finger. I've heard people say that they were in so much pain that they were delirious. I could never understand that until this happened to me. It was simply unimaginable.

I got out of bed and the only thing I could do was walk in a circle…for forty-five minutes. This is why I can now understand when someone says they were delirious with pain. I was not in my right mind. I did not know why I was walking in a circle and I couldn't stop. While walking, I called out for the Lord to take the pain way. "Take it away Lord, take it away!" I must have said that a thousand times. I didn't know what to do. That's what this type of pain will do to you. It leaves you senseless, delirious, and incapable of doing anything to help yourself. I didn't know what was happening, yet I wasn't afraid. I still believed that it wasn't a heart attack, but I couldn't explain what it was.

After forty-five minutes of walking in a circle that couldn't have been more than three feet in diameter, crying, and calling out to the Lord, I was finally able to see that I needed to do something. I needed help but I couldn't stop walking in that circle. I felt very out of control in my motions. My daughter was sleeping and I didn't want to wake her because she had school the next morning. (Again, a mother putting everyone's needs above her own.) I came to realize that I had no other option but to call out to her and hope she would hear me. I could not get my motor skills together enough to walk from the back of the house to her room up front. She did hear me and I thanked God for that!

My poor baby took one look at me, turned, and walked out of my room. She never said a word, so I wasn't quite sure what she was about to do. She went straight to the phone and called her cousin, my niece. I'm so proud of how calm my daughter was able to be in the midst of me losing my mind. What she saw that night she had never seen before. My hope for her is that she never has to witness anyone suffer like that again.

In hindsight, there is one thing from that night that I am glad about. Had this happened prior to me accepting Christ, my daughter would have witnessed something altogether different. Instead of praying my way through, I would have cursed my way through. Thank God that's no longer me. *"If any man be in Christ he is a new creature. Old things are passed away, behold all things become new" (II Corinthians 5:17)*. I am grateful that God extended enough grace to me for me to come into the new woman I am. I am thankful that in my most trying of times my daughter saw and heard me call upon the Lord for help. There may come a point in her life when she encounters something she feels she cannot bear and I pray that she will reflect back to that night and call upon the Lord for help, as well.

My niece only lived five minutes from us so she arrived at the house very quickly. I think what she saw shocked her, but like my daughter, she was able to push beyond what she was seeing and react properly to the situation. The two of them had to help me get dressed and put my shoes on. I don't think there was a moment I stopped praying out loud, continually saying "Take it away Lord, take it away." Those words are forever etched in my mind. I didn't know what else to do but seek His help. As my niece drove to the hospital, I repeated my prayer incessantly. For a few brief minutes, just before we arrived at the hospital, the pain vanished. What in the world was going on? I could not wrap my brain around what was happening to me. How could something so terribly painful be there one second, last for solid periods of time, and then just go away? I was completely perplexed.

When we arrived at the hospital, I was in okay shape until they put me in a wheelchair to take me to the exam room. I don't know what wrong move I made, but something brought the pain flooding back. "Take it away Lord, take it away", started all over again.

At some points, I can remember being so tired and worn out that although I was saying it, my voice was low and faint. My energy was fading away, and just as I felt I had to keep walking in a circle I felt I had to keep saying this. I needed the Lord to hear me and He had to help me!

The television show *House* was not one of my favorites, but I am familiar with it. The main character is a bit crass and desensitized for my taste. If I say I've watched the show five times, that's probably an over estimate. From the couple times I did watch it, I know there is a lot of consulting that goes on. Doctors, interns, and the like all stand around a patient's bedside and hypothesize about what may be the issue. Well, the cameras should have been rolling that night in the ER because that is exactly the scene that played out in my exam room. They thought I could be having a heart attack, so they gave me nitro glycerin tablets that fizzed under my tongue. A heart attack was not what I was having and I tried to tell them that.

It all fell on deaf ears. I can't even count the number of nitro pills I had that night, but I was too exhausted to refuse any of them. What they did know was that I was in extreme pain because that was quite obvious. They gave me an IV of morphine. A mobile X-ray machine was brought in to take chest x-rays while I sat up in the bed. I can't even remember all the other things that were done or given to me. What I do remember was that I started to feel a little better. I couldn't tell if it was from the morphine or not. I was just thankful for the relief. Yet, a very short while later (meaning minutes, not hours), a huge wave of pain hit me. This is where the cameras should have been rolling again, as if on *House*. As I sat on the bed screaming from this unexplainable thing that was terrorizing me, I looked at the foot of my bed to see several men in white doctor coats standing there. "She's still in pain after everything we have given her", is what I heard one of them say to the others. The statement was made more in the way of a question of disbelief than anything else. It was as if they were shocked that I was feeling anything after the amount of pain killers that had been pumped through my IV. They were truly baffled at what was plaguing me.

There isn't much more about that late evening/early morning that I remember. I don't recall being discharged from the hospital, getting back in my niece's car or, for that matter, getting home and back in my bed. Frankly, the next few days are still a blur. With the help of family, friends, and receipts from hospitals, here is what I have been able to piece together. I went to the ER that night, was treated (drugged up), and released. I went back to the ER sometime the next day. At that point, I was admitted to the hospital and kept for two days. During that time various tests were done and I stayed heavily medicated. From the results of an MRI, I was told that I had degenerative disc disease, informed that I should follow up with a specialist, and released. I have a few vague memories from my two-day stay, mostly being wheeled around the hospital as I was being taken for diagnostic tests. The day after being released, I went back to the ER because I just couldn't take the pain.

Many things transpired in the days that followed, but even with the assistance of others it is hard to put all the pieces together in retrospect. One thing is for certain, the diagnosis I received was not correct. I did not have degenerative disc disease. Upon visiting the neurologist and another MRI being done by his office, it clearly showed that I had two discs in my neck that had slipped out of place. One of them was pressing on a nerve and that is what had been causing the extreme pain. There is no amount of medication that makes nerve pain go away. The only thing that helps is to take the pressure off the nerve, which could mean surgery.

I was grateful to finally have an understanding of what was going on with me. For a moment, however, I was extremely frustrated that three trips to the ER, being seen by countless doctors, and an MRI being done in the hospital was not sufficient to find this out. I couldn't allow myself to stay frustrated for long though. It was now time to focus on a resolution. When the neurologist gave me the real diagnosis, my only question was "What will you have to do to fix this?" He explained the procedure to me in great detail.

Anterior Cervical Discectomy with Fusion was his answer. I have to admit that I was not at all enthused about the prospect of him having to cut my neck open, remove two discs, replace them with metal pieces, and then fuse three vertebrae together with a metal plate secured with six screws. I may not have been enthused about it but I can promise you that I signed up for it without hesitation. Whatever needed to be done to ensure I would not have to relive that indescribable pain again is what I was going to do. The only downside seemed to be that I would have to wait a few weeks before his schedule allowed for the surgery.

The Son I Never Had

As a young girl, whenever I imagined what my adult life would be like, especially in terms of having my own family, I always visualized having a son first and then a daughter. That's how it was in our house when I grew up. My brother is older than me and it was just the two of us. That was how I saw my future family being structured. Of course, as we learn later in life, we don't get to dictate much of how those things unfold. As such, my only legal child is my daughter.

But, from the time I was in my early twenties up until this very day, the Lord has placed one child after another in my life. It's been an interesting journey with the young ones I call, "my babies".

Regardless of how old they are, I still refer to them that way. I used to wonder why He brought them into my life, but I don't anymore. I enjoy the challenge of trying to add value to their lives.

Nurturing each one of them has been my absolute pleasure. Each of these relationships has presented its own unique experience. I've always found it to be interesting that I can tell right away when a young person is destined to be one of "my babies". There is a level of comfort I have with them immediately, almost as if they were already a part of my family. I feel a desire to pull them close to me. The first few were all girls and then the Lord changed things up and sent a boy. Actually, by the time our paths crossed he was already a young man. By way of a basketball scholarship, he was attending the local community college when he came into the family fold. This was foreign territory for me. I had never parented a boy before. When he came into my life, he was much older than the girls when they had come along. I had no idea how to parent a half-grown man. Yet, because of his background, he desperately needed parenting and needed to be part of a family. It was made clear to me shortly after our meeting that he was supposed to be part of mine. He didn't ask for it but I knew what the Lord had put on my heart to do. Weaving him into the fabric of our family was a gradual process. You don't meet someone today and say, "Would you like to be my son?"

By all accounts, he should have been a statistic by the time we met. His childhood was less than desirable. In fact, his childhood could be classified as unstable. He lived with friends, family, team mates, coaches, and anyone he could along the way. His father died when he was a young boy. His mother was not able to be in his life for periods of time when he was young, and he had one brother in jail. If you've ever seen the movie **Blind Side** you have a good idea of his life as a child. When that movie came out, we went to see it as a family. I was able to relate a great deal to Sandra Bullock's character as a mother who had taken in a child who was not her own. I had become quite protective over him, in a motherly kind of way, just as she became over the young man she took into her family. There were many similarities between our family situation and the one that we watched play out on the theater screen.

All odds were against him just as they were against Michael Oher, the main character in **Blind Side,** yet he seemed determined to succeed. Part of succeeding meant developing survival techniques. Michael Oher was depicted as shy in the movie. My son's personality is the opposite. He has a magnetic personality which gives him favor with people. As a young boy, I think he learned to use that to his advantage.

After graduating from the community college, he was blessed to receive another scholarship that would allow him to finish his education at a four-year university in another state. He wasn't scheduled to go there until the Fall. The summer months left him homeless…literally. By this time, I had been helping him with things like groceries, inviting him over for family dinners, etc. Living with my daughter and I was not something that I had anticipated, but it was hard for me to think about someone I cared for being homeless. He had proven to be a resourceful young man (survival technique), so I knew he would end up somewhere safe for those in between months if I did not take him in. Somehow the thought of him being "somewhere" was not good enough. I wanted him to have more. He was becoming family so I wanted him to be with family.

He did not have much of a father figure growing up, so I thought it would be a good idea to try and provide one for him for the summer. I asked a male family member of mine to provide a place for him to stay for a couple of months until he left for college. I was committed to helping this young man but I knew it was asking a lot of someone else to make the same level of commitment. My desire to give him a temporary father figure did not pan out, so I asked if he wanted to stay with me until he left for college. He gladly agreed and from that point on, in my heart, he became the son I never had. When he initially moved in, things were a little awkward at times.

He was so independent and accustomed to coming and going as he pleased. I had house rules, as all moms do. I felt responsible for him since he was living with me. He was not used to anyone caring much about where he went, when he'd be back, or even who he was with. I was not used to someone living in my home and thinking it was okay to walk out the door and not say anything, not even "good-bye" or "see you later." The new living arrangement certainly came with growing pains.

Even with the growing pains, there was plenty of family fun and bonding that took place. For the first time in years, he had a mom that was concerned about preparing meals for her family. For the first time ever, he had a little sister to look after and help care for.

We went to church as a family, and for as much as my schedule would allow, we did weekend activities together. He could now look forward to birthdays and Christmases knowing that he would be remembered and acknowledged by people who loved him.

I had recently separated from my first husband and could only afford a two-bedroom apartment at the time. There were three of us living in the space that I considered small compared to the house my daughter and I moved from. We made it work the best we could. My daughter was so young then that she slept in my bed more often than not. My new, unofficially adopted son would then sleep in her room or on the sofa in the living room. When he left to start the Fall semester at the university, I remember promising him that when he came home the next time, I would have a house and he would have his own room.

The Lord blessed me to be able to keep that promise. When he returned from school, we had moved from the apartment into a house and he indeed did have his own bedroom. He told me that he had never had his own room before and I was stunned. Considering his background, I probably should not have been, but I was. I was sad for him. Even sadder was the Christmas before my husband and I separated. We invited him to spend Christmas Eve and Christmas Day with us. Had we not, he would have been by himself and that was simply unacceptable to me. I recall asking my husband to buy this young man some Christmas presents. I didn't know what to get him but I wanted to be sure that while we were opening our gifts Christmas morning, he would have something to open as well. I didn't want him to feel left out. I believe my husband purchased a total of five gifts for him. I couldn't tell you now what any of them were and I'm not sure that it matters. He was touched and said, "These five gifts are more than I got in the last five years combined."

The more I learned about him the more my heart broke for him, and the more I admired him as well. He was purposeful about succeeding beyond his circumstances and I wanted to help him. When we met him, he had been on his own for quite some time. He worked to cover expenses the scholarship did not provide for and he did his best to keep a reliable means of transportation so he could work. His grades were more than good when you consider all of the distractions that could have pulled his attention away. He was focused on rising above his past and I applauded him for that.

Once the Fall semester started and basketball season was underway, I made plans for my daughter and I to go visit him. We had never seen him play basketball, but to hear him tell the story, he was quite good, of course! It was a long drive to the Carolinas but it was worth every minute on the road. Our visit was a surprise to him and the look on his face when we came into the gymnasium was priceless. He picked up my daughter, who he was now calling his little sister, and gave her a huge hug and she hugged him back just as tight. I believe it was on that trip I became his "mom" and he became my "son" by titles. He was proud to introduce his mom and sister to his teammates, friends, and coaches. It was during that trip I felt we would be family forever.

Each Mother's Day and birthday my son would find the most incredible cards. They were so touching and would often make me cry. He seemed to have a knack for picking out cards that truly spoke to our relationship. He seemed grateful that I was attempting to give him something that, up until we met, he had not known much about before – family. As with the girls the Lord had placed in my life, I was grateful He chose me to fill the void this young man had as a result of this childhood. He is an interesting young man and I was enjoying having him in the family, and as my son.

As time went by, we tried to find our comfort zone as a family unit. His being away at college made it a little challenging. We only lived together as a family during breaks and summer vacations. It was hard to find our footing with the inconsistency of the living arrangement. Consequently, there were many ups and downs the following years. It seemed that no matter what I did or tried to do, he never felt secure in his place within the family. We had several misunderstandings that seemed to result because I treated him like one of my children. Since he was unfamiliar with family dynamics, he felt I treated him differently because he was not my actual son. This was not at all true. I have learned, however, that it is hard to combat someone's perception. It is their reality.

Our relationship became a turbulent roller-coaster. There were good times sprinkled throughout, as well as periods of time when we did not see him because he was upset with me and wouldn't come around. When times were good, they were very good. We would laugh and talk, and the three of us would even go on family vacations. He would tell me I was not only a mother to him, but a friend as well because we could talk freely about anything.

When times were bad, they were quite bad. He would get upset about things he perceived I did to him. No amount of explaining could get him to think any differently. It was a painful process. My heart was always in the right place, so it hurt deeply when he felt I treated him differently. I wondered if things would ever level out. I will admit, there were times I would ask the Lord "do I still have to do this?" I felt I had extended myself to this young man in a pure, well-meaning way and accepted him into my family. Along the way, there were times I felt unappreciated, used, and disrespected. Did I still have to subject myself to that? Because the bad times were so terribly bad, I wondered if our relationship was meant to last for only a season, more so than a lifetime. Had it been the Lord's plan all along for me to be there just to help him with his college years? Each time I asked, the Lord would tell me to continue trying. "Show him what family means," the Lord said. No matter how deflated I sometimes felt in my spirit about the relationship, I stayed obedient to what the Lord had put in my heart to do. Besides that, I never wanted him out of my life. I was just frustrated and at a loss for what to do. I hadn't experienced challenges like this with any of the girls. I can't tell you how many times I prayed and asked for guidance. God said, "Keep trying". All families go through challenges. Ours was sure to have them, considering we came together as adults with pre-established ideas that had been formed from such different backgrounds and life experiences. Regardless, he was my son and no matter how frustrated I was at times, I continued on.

One evening he asked me, "Why do you keep letting me come back after the things I did?" He didn't speak of any specific thing he had done. I guess he felt I knew. I explained to him that family doesn't give up on family. Every family has their problems and challenges.

At the end of the day, however, if my family is in need and I'm in a position to help, that's what I'm going to do. Our relationship had been unbalanced for a long time. I constantly gave and he constantly received. I attribute that to the survival skills he had to learn when he was on his own as a young adult. Although I understood where those tendencies grew from, my goal was to help him see he was no longer alone. He didn't have to always operate in survival mode. I wanted him to see it was now safe to let his defenses down. He had a family now; A Forever Family. My heart's desire was to see him rest comfortably in that and not feel like he had to rebel against it.

Whats In A Name

The date of my surgery was still a couple weeks away. The intense pain from the disc laying on a nerve had begun to subside. According to the doctor, this was due to the anti-inflammatory I had been taking, as well as the amount of rest I was able to get the past several weeks. To be clear, there was not a lot of 'rest' during this period of time. It was more like idleness. There was not much I was physically able to do. Regardless of the reasons, I was happy to be over that phase of my condition. The unfortunate part was something new was happening. Once the pain lessened, an equally intense form of achiness set in. From my left elbow, down my forearm, and all through the top of the hand I ached. I've never had a broken bone in my body but I imagined this must be what one felt like. This is the only way I know to describe the feeling. Nothing soothed it. I tried an ice pack, and then alternated with a heating pad; neither worked. I rubbed my arm and hand constantly but that didn't help either. The pain pills no longer provided any relief. I remember putting my arm in a sling as a last resort. I thought, "If I can just keep it still, it won't hurt". Nothing I tried to alleviate my aches worked and it drove me insane! I was at a loss for what to do.

During one of our daily phone conversations, I told my mom how I had been praying for the achiness to go away but it only seemed to get worse. I didn't understand why my prayers weren't being answered this time. If anything, I had more faith in God's abilities now than ever before because of the way He had blessed me earlier in the year. When I was in pain then and called on Him for help, He helped me. I couldn't stop wondering why He wasn't helping me now. I was so uncomfortable that I couldn't rest.

My mom asked me if I was praying the right way. "The right way! What does that mean?" I asked. I never heard there was a wrong way to pray. She said, "Call the spirit by its name and command it to flee, in the name of Jesus, and it will have to obey". I believed that she was right. I believe there are some forces of darkness that will bother us until we recognize exactly who they are and command them to flee! The reminder from my mom gave me renewed hope that I would not suffer much longer with the achy condition.

In hindsight, it seems funny to me that I would forget the importance of a name. As a parent, I've tried to teach my daughter (and my other babies) many things to help along the way of life. Be kind, honest, and compassionate. My goal was to relay, we are known by our name. Over the years, I have asked my daughter to ponder this question: "when someone hears your name, what comes to their mind?" I wanted her to think about what her named carried. My prayer for her, and all the other special kids in my life, is that they would conduct themselves in such a way that their names would be synonymous with respect, love, generosity and kindness. How could I then forget that power is synonymous with the name Jesus? I had not been using the power available to me through His name! Thank God for my mother and her reminder. If you can believe there is power in the name of Jesus, you have the faith you need to survive. Of our own strength, we might be able to be conquerors, but it is with Him and through Him that we can be MORE than conquerors over the challenges that come our way. I was so excited! My mom had given me the rejuvenation I needed to continue fighting! When we finished talking that day, I remembered a bottle of anointed oil I kept in the bathroom cabinet. My dear friend, Ms. Bernie gave it to me. She and I met a few years back while standing at the self-service photo machines in CVS. We struck up a forty-five minute conversation. In that time, we found it amazing the number of things we had in common even though we were years apart in age. We exchanged phone numbers that day and grew to be quite close. We both agreed it was an ordained encounter.

I was familiar with the concept of anointed oil when Ms. Bernie gave it to me, but I had never used any myself. I had only seen Pastors use oil during church services while blessing people. I imagined there should be a purifying process before using the oil, so before I picked up the bottle, I washed my hands. Her Bishop had already blessed the oil, but I said my own prayer before I opened the bottle. I cradled it in the palm of my right hand and asked the Lord to allow the oil to accomplish the task I believed it would. I'm not sure a prayer was necessary but it was in my heart to say one, so I did. Once my prayer was sent and sealed with "in the name of Jesus", I dabbed the oil on the left side of my chest, shoulder, arm, hand, and index finger. While doing this, I thanked Jesus in advance for my healing and then started walking. I walked, prayed, and called those spirits out of my body by their names. "Spirit of achiness, in the name of Jesus, you must flee from my body! In the name of Jesus, spirit of discomfort, you must flee from my body!" In a matter-of-fact manner, I reminded each of them, "My body is God's temple. You do not belong here. I command you to flee from me, my body, and my house! In the name of Jesus, you will not find rest in any other soul I care about, especially those living in my house!" It is important to remember that when a spirit obeys (which it has to) and leaves one body, it will look for somewhere to go. I decreed and declared wherever they went, it wouldn't be into anyone I loved! I walked in faith. I prayed in faith. I spoke healing in faith. When I got tired, I sat for a short while and then resumed my march…up and down the hallway, repeating my prayer. For three days, I walked the hallway of my house from the front door to the back door. While walking, I called out the painful, achy spirits that were inhabiting my body. Doing this was a true expression of faith on my part. Although I had not done this before, I believed that it would work. I needed to believe it would work. That's what faith is all about; believing in something that we don't see, can't explain, or even understand.

I can't say I experienced some sensational feeling when the spirits fled. While walking on the third day, I noticed at one point I no longer ached. I was no longer in pain, nor was I uncomfortable. This was incredible and yet another opportunity to praise the Lord! After working through my excitement, I grabbed the phone and called my mom. I couldn't wait to tell her about this. How could I NOT tell someone? Everyone! I was in awe of what had taken place, once again. This was all new to me. At no time in my life before 2013 could I remember yielding to the power in the name Jesus in such a way. How could I, an average ordinary person, be able to pray like this and see such real results? It was only by faith in believing that it was possible to begin with. *Mark 11:24 "Therefore I say unto you, whatsoever ye desire, when ye pray, believe that ye receive them, and ye shall have them."* There may be some who will read this and doubt what I am saying and I understand. I doubted at one time, as well. That's why I feel so strongly about sharing these details. It is important for people to know God wants us to use the power we have through His son Jesus in our lives. It's an opportunity to give Him glory and honor, as well as show others that He is real and be able to live our best life possible!

After I called and shared the good news with my mom, I called a few other people. There were some who joined me in praise. There were some who listened but didn't comment much, if at all. Then there was one or two who didn't know how to respond or what to say. My prayer is that the Lord used all those moments to let each person know if He did it for me, He can do it for them too. They just need to believe and have faith in Him.

Over the years, I struggled with believing He would do 'it' for me. Whatever 'it' may have been at the time (peace of mind, a job, a relationship, a new home, etc.) My mind could not compute why He would do anything for me. I always knew that He was more than capable of doing anything He chose to, but I doubted He would do anything for me. I saw Him bless people around me but couldn't comprehend why He would bless me. This is where we make our greatest mistake. God longs to be good to us. Often times, we have to get out of His way by removing doubt and condemnation in our minds.

As if at the theater, I played out every mistake of my life on the movie screen in my head. Thoughts like, "Why would God bless me after what I did?" or "Why would He answer my prayer after what I said?" ran through my mind often, when it came time to seek Him. I was good at convincing myself that I was not worthy of His goodness. The reality is I am not worthy, but that simply speaks to how great He is. Despite my shortcomings and failures, He does want to help me and always has wanted to. I just had to get out of His way with my negative thoughts. When we begin to think like He thinks about us, life gets better. The only way we can begin the process of thinking like Him is to know what the word says. When it comes to condemnation in particular, I love what the Bible says to counter our negative mindset:

1) *"Let the redeemed of the Lord say so..." Psalm 107:2* We are not what we have done. Once we've confessed and repented, it's over. Let it go. Move on. The Lord has. *Hebrews 8:12 "For I will be merciful to their unrighteousness, and their sins and their iniquities will I remember no more."* If the Lord, your God, is not thinking on what you did (past tense emphasized), then why are you? Why was I?

2) *1 Peter 2:9-10 "But ye are a chosen generation, a royal priesthood, an holy nation, a peculiar people; that ye should shew forth the praises of him who hath called you out of darkness into his marvelous light: Which in time past were not a people, but are now the people of God: which had not obtained mercy, but now have obtained mercy."* I absolutely love this verse! Royalty; that's how God sees us even after the scripture acknowledges that He called us out of darkness (sin). So, even after knowing all that we did, He still sees us as His chosen generation and reminds us of the mercy that has been shown to us. If He can be merciful to us, surely we can be to ourselves. These are the reasons why we have to work hard to rebuke condemnation. God is not condemning us so we have to stop condemning ourselves. *"There is therefore now no condemnation to them which are in Christ Jesus, who walk not after the flesh, but after the Spirit." Romans 8:1*

Despite the fact that I was in one of the toughest places of my life, I was beginning to realize, I had so much to be grateful for. The Lord was proving Himself to be ever-present in my life during the challenges at hand. That alone was something to be extremely grateful for. My brother, however, was another. For reasons that no longer matter, he and I had grown apart the past couple of years. The distance between us was a very sad thing for me, and for him too, I believe. We had always been so close. We are only eighteen months apart so we are obviously close in age. At one time, we were much closer at heart. I jokingly tell people we were telepathic when we were younger. During our college years, if I thought about him for a few minutes, he would call and vice versa. When I got married and moved away, it wouldn't surprise me if we talked on the phone every day for the first year.

But then life happened and we drifted apart. Yet, when I was in the time of my greatest need, he drove twelve hours with his toddler in tow to come and see about me. I think he arrived somewhere around the second or third trip to the emergency room. Walking into my home after returning from the ER and seeing my brother in the kitchen making food for my family and me was something I will never forget. I may have been heavily medicated at the time but I remember that clearly. That's how significant it was to me. It was beyond special. It was cleansing. The issues we had no longer mattered. For so long, I had wanted to talk with him about how far off track we had gotten. Now, it simply didn't matter to me. When you are confronted with life-altering circumstances, things can be put into perspective very quickly. Things you previously thought were important become so unimportant. He was there with me and that was important. He helped me find a doctor to do my surgery. That was important. I could see and feel his concern. That was important. My brother stayed for a few days until things were a bit more stable and I greatly appreciated all that he did during his visit. There are still huge gaps in my memory from that time frame, but one thing I do know is I was well taken care of when he was there. The weeks following my brother's departure were tolerable but I became anxious for the surgery. Now that an accurate diagnosis had been made, I wanted it corrected so life could resume as normal. I didn't want to be home anymore. I wanted to be well so I could go back to work. I didn't want to feel incapable of taking care of my family anymore. My friends and family had been wonderful by pitching in with cooking and running errands, but I wanted to be self-sufficient again. I wanted to be off all the medications I was taking. It had almost been a full month of taking multiple pills a day. None of this would be possible until after the surgery which made me quite anxious for February 21st to come.

On the day before the surgery, instead of being excited the time had finally come, I experienced something different altogether. I felt very alone and battled a strong spirit of fear. Frequently throughout the day I found myself thinking, "What if I don't make it through the surgery tomorrow?", "After all, he is cutting my throat.", "What if he accidentally hits an artery?" I tortured myself all day with thoughts like that. "Would this be the last day I would see my family?" I wanted to spend quality time with them the evening before my surgery but I also didn't want them to know how worried I was becoming. I didn't want them to see me concerned and think they had reason to be concerned. I would be going in for surgery in the morning and my daughter would be going to school. I didn't want her to stress so I tried hard to be 'okay' that day. I am a woman of faith, but I am also a human being made of flesh, blood, and emotions. That day, for the first time, I felt like I had to make a conscientious decision and choose to be one or the other – a woman of faith or a human being. It seemed strange that I felt there was a choice to make, but it was in my best interest to do so. Frankly, I wasn't sure which one was winning, but after a while I knew the woman of faith needed to take the lead. I had been letting my mind entertain all sorts of thoughts and that needed to stop. I called a few people who I knew would help get me back on track. Doing that was the best decision I made that day. They helped fortify my faith by reminding me that I still have purpose. That was probably the most significant thing said to me that day. My purpose had not yet been fulfilled and God is faithful to finish what He starts. That was what I needed to hear so I received the message gladly!

I was up late that night talking with friends and family members, and making sure I had things in place for the next few days. I anticipated when I came home from the hospital all I would want to do is rest. Even though it would be outpatient surgery, it was still major and would be traumatic to my body. The next morning, February 21st, I had to be at the hospital at 5am. for a surgery time of 7am. Skipping over the details, I will just say that my surgery ended up being at 10am. Better yet, let's not skip over the details because the details will help establish my state of mind.

It was early on a Thursday morning. I had been dropped off at the hospital by my niece, and was anxious for my surgery because I wanted it to be over. This had been going on now for over a month. I was tired, frustrated, and at points along the way, downright miserable. Here I was at the hospital to have a very serious surgery, yet I was completely by myself and wondered, "How'd that happen?" To be at this age/stage in life and have no one by my side was a painful realization by itself. This was certainly not how I pictured my life to have turned out. Beyond that, I didn't even want to be there because I surely didn't want to be going through any of this. But, if I had to be I certainly did not want to be there alone during the five hour wait. I imagined how wonderful it would have been to have someone there with me, reassuring me that things would be fine. There were a lot of people waiting by their phones for an update when the procedure was over, but there was not one soul physically there with me. This was turning out to be the absolute loneliest day of my life.

For five very long hours, I laid there in a pre-op cubicle. As cold as it was in the hospital there was no way I was comfortable, no matter how many blankets they gave me. On top of that, they had already prepped me for the IV that would administer the necessary medicines through my veins. I had the tube stuck in the top of my right hand, ready and waiting. It didn't necessarily hurt but it was uncomfortable. It made me feel as if I should limit my movements to avoid it from moving. The less I moved, the less I felt it. The less I felt it, the less likely I thought it would be to come loose which, if it did come loose, I knew it would hurt. On top of all that, I hadn't eaten anything or had even a sip of water since before midnight. Needless to say, none of the circumstances of that day would be used to describe my preferred situation. By 7am I wondered when the show would start. By 9am, I wondered if they had forgotten about me! At last…10am rolled around and they were finally ready to take me into the operating room. Little did they know, I was beyond ready.

Looking back I can see now that the Lord was with me, so I wasn't alone as I thought or may have felt. For all the negative that I acknowledged about my situation that morning, I was at peace. It was the peace of God that was with me that morning. There is no other explanation to satisfy the natural mind as to how I could lay there on what amounted to a gurney for five hours without food or water, no one to talk to, and just wait. Not only was I able to wait, but I waited patiently. And to keep it real, those close to me know that patience has been my life-long struggle. But what could I do? Nothing! There was nothing about this morning that was in my control. Yet, I remained at peace which does pass all levels of understanding for me. Reflecting back, I recall being content. I had submitted my very being to the will of the Lord. Whatever was going to happen was going to happen whether I was impatient about it or content with it. I had been in unfamiliar territory during those five hours of waiting. I had been completely at peace. Frankly, I couldn't understand it myself!

"And the peace of God which passes all understanding shall keep our hearts and minds through Christ Jesus." (Philippians 4:7). For years, I have been able to quote this scripture but somehow the true meaning of it had eluded me for just as long. I could never quite grasp the part that says "passes all understanding". What was there to understand? You either had the peace of God or you didn't, right? Until this particular day, I thought that I did. Let me tell you though, there is a type of peace that you really just can't explain even when you have found it. It is hard to put into words or comprehend with our natural minds. On the day of my operation, I finally knew the peace this scripture refers to. You become 'okay' with the circumstances around you because you get to a place where you know, trust, and believe that God is in control. It seems funny to me that it would happen at a time like this, but it did. But then again, maybe it is only at times like these that it can happen; when you're in a situation to truly choose who is in control of your life – you or God (the one who created you and knew you from the beginning of time).

We can be so hard on ourselves. It is important on any journey we take to stop once in a while and look at how far we've come. Doing so gives us encouragement to keep moving forward. Although, I certainly was not happy to wait as long as I did that morning, I realized how much I've come in my walk with Christ over the years. The old me would have stressed and complained after 7am (honestly, more like 6am). The nurses would have known me well, but not for any good reason. By the time they wheeled me into the operating room, everyone on duty would have heard of me because the old me would not have been pleased to have been misled and made to wait so long. I would have been angry and they would have known it. Thank God for His grace that has allowed me to grow. Besides that, who wants to agitate everyone who is assisting the surgeon who is about to cut your neck open? Not me, that was for sure.

Waiting was not easy to do, not easy at all. I had to put forth an effort. While waiting, I focused on all of the good things instead of focusing on the delay. *"Finally, brethren, whatsoever things are true, whatsoever things are honest, whatsoever things are just, whatsoever things are pure, whatsoever things are lovely, whatsoever things are of good report; if there be any virtue, and if there be any praise, think on these things." Philippians 4:8* That's what I had to do. I had to think on all the good things, and in reality there was a lot to be grateful for, to look forward to, and to be happy about. After the surgery, I would no longer have any physical limitations. And though I may not have had anyone there at the hospital with me, my family would be waiting for me when I got home. Other family and friends would be coming by to check on me, they would call, and they would send cards of encouragement. I would also be able to go back to work, which I had been longing to do. No matter how bad something seems or feels, if we can pull ourselves out of our feelings long enough, we can see our situation more objectively and realize that we are still blessed!

I remember being excited when my doctor finally came in to let me know they were ready for the surgery. He went over a few things and before I knew it, I was being wheeled down the hall, headed for the operating room. I wasn't nervous. Everyone had been very nice all morning and my doctor was confident. I consider him a funny man, although many can't appreciate his bedside manner. We could always find something to laugh about, and that morning was no exception. The joke of the day was how much longer my neck was than the guy he operated on before me. My long neck would give him plenty of room to work he said, and we both chuckled. As I was being lifted from the gurney to the operating table, I remember asking questions. I wondered if all patients did that or if it was just me. "Can I see what you're going to put in me?" I asked. They showed me the titanium pieces that would replace the discs. They looked like small cubes from what I recall. The plate which would be used to fuse the bones together was flat and funny shaped. I didn't see the screws that would be used to attach the plate to the vertebrae, but screws were screws, I imagined. After that they, stopped answering my questions. This wasn't because they were being rude; they knew that any second now I was about to drift off to sleep because of the medicine that was just put into my IV. The last thing I remember was the anesthesiologist putting the mask over my nose and mouth…while I was still trying to talk to all of them! When I woke up in the recovery room, I remember being very alert and aware of everything immediately. The first thing that I recognized was the pain I felt across my chest from shoulder to shoulder. This surprised me because I didn't have pain from shoulder to shoulder before the surgery, so why now? In typical fashion, I started asking questions again. I was told that, in order for them to secure me properly, allowing the surgeon to safely make the incision in the front of my throat, they had to strap me down as flat and tight as possible. Now it made sense. Muscles had been stretched that I never knew I had! Then it dawned on me, I'm talking! For some reason I didn't expect to be able to do that right after surgery, but it was indeed a blessing.

Because I was talking, however, I noticed how sore my throat felt. That was apparently from the tube that had been down my throat during the operation.

When it was removed it left my throat feeling a little raw. My neck was numb; I simply didn't feel it. If it weren't for the huge bandage on the front of my neck I wouldn't have known that anything had been done to it. There was no feeling there.

What I did feel was the tip of my left index finger. Because one of the discs had been pressing on a particular nerve for such a long period of time, I had lost feeling in that finger. It was amazing to me that feeling had been restored instantly. It had been numb for so long but now I could feel it again. I was being restored back to my healthy self and was grateful and excited! When I recognize a blessing of the Lord, I praise Him without hesitation. So, while still in the recovery room I was rejoicing on the inside, as well as outwardly, for the blessing I had received. "Praise the Lord and thank you Jesus" came out of my mouth several times. I remember even laughing in amazement. He can do anything He chooses to do and that was shown to me again that day. My doctor had been confident the surgery would restore the feeling in my finger again, but he could not say exactly when. The fact that it was so immediate was truly amazing.

I was ALIVE. I was WELL. I was going HOME. I felt like doing a happy dance! When I was discharged, one of my friends picked me up from the hospital and took me home. I was still in awe that I could speak. Thinking back, I never asked the doctor what I could expect after surgery in terms of that. During a pre-op appointment the nurses did discuss appropriate after-surgery foods with me. I was told to stock up on all cold, easy-to-swallow foods. They said my throat would burn so badly after surgery that I would only be able to tolerate foods such as Jello, pudding, and yogurt. I love cottage cheese but they told me that would probably be too difficult for me to swallow. I heeded to their advice and, before the surgery, stocked the refrigerator with all of the things they suggested.

I wanted to be prepared. Well, when you have Dr. Jesus on your side, things don't go the way people expect. Thanks to a blessing from my neighbors, I was able to enjoy dinner from Boston Market at 7pm that night! I was released from the hospital at 5pm and was eating rotisserie chicken, steamed veggies, and macaroni and cheese for dinner two hours later! Needless to say, much of the cold, snack foods I had purchased went to waste over the following weeks. I couldn't believe how good I felt after having something so significant done in that area of my body. Actually, I was surprised this was out-patient surgery. When it was all said and done, I was much stronger than I thought I would be when I left the hospital. When I got home I felt great but did need rest. I had been up late the night before the surgery and had to be up very early the morning of. I was tired, but in excellent shape considering my operation. After eating dinner, I looked forward to a peaceful night of sleep. I had much to catch up on in that department. The unfortunate part is there would be no rest for me the next two days. At certain times, I thought I was operating on fumes of energy, not actual energy. But I did what I had to do.

CHAPTER 6

A Mother's Prayer

Prior to my surgery, my son committed to being the person who would stay at my home and help me through the recovery process. We had no idea how I would feel afterwards, or what I would be able to do and not do, but we were prepared with a plan. Sadly, a few days before my surgery, he blew out his knee playing basketball. He had to have surgery two days before me and I ended up being his caregiver instead of him being mine. So much for plans!

Although, I do consider my surgery to have been major because of the location and risk factors involved, it turned out his was much more painful and debilitating afterwards. Keeping him as comfortable as possible became my number one priority. The bedroom he had in my home was a fairly small one and did not have a television at the time. I moved out of my bedroom and let him have it while he was in recovery. He needed to have room to maneuver. Being in a small space at over 6' tall and on crutches was not going to work. He was only supposed to get up when absolutely necessary which meant he would be spending a lot of time in bed. My room was much larger in size, had a larger bathroom to maneuver around, and there was a TV mounted on the wall. It seemed like the best location for him during his recuperation. The den became my room and I slept on the sofa. The den is next to my bedroom so this allowed me to be close enough to hear him if he called for help during the night. It was definitely a sacrifice of my comfort, but mothers do what they have to for their kids.

Even though I was extremely tired when I came home from the hospital the day of my operation, I was up all night helping him. He needed ice on and off his knee every 20 minutes. My daughter had school so there was no way I was going to have her up through the night doing this. She needed her rest so she would be able to focus and concentrate in class.

Other than cat naps during the day, I can't say I rested or slept much the first 48 hours after my surgery. He needed me though. What was I to do? After the second sleepless night I tried to hire a caregiver to come and assist us through the evening. On such short notice, I was not able to find one I could afford. I was absolutely exhausted. Have you ever felt so tired and depleted of energy that all you could do was cry? That's where I was.

Thankfully, after that second night he seemed to not need the ice packs as much as before, which allowed me to rest in the evenings.

I was grateful for that. Grateful that his evenings were becoming less painful and grateful for the opportunity I now had to rest.

His recovery took precedence over mine. He was bed-ridden, I was not. Now that the pressure had been taken off of the nerve, I had full use of both arms and hands again. Thank God for that because I needed to be able-bodied now. After almost two months of not being able to cook, clean, or drive, I had to get back in the saddle, quickly. He had to be off his knee for an extended period of time.

This meant it was up to me to ensure he had meals so he was not taking pain medicine on an empty stomach. Some days, I joked about how much I was catering to him. Until he was able to move about on his own, each day, three times a day, I would carry a tray of food into the room for him - breakfast, lunch, and dinner. I'm pretty sure he enjoyed the attention and the spoiling. In a matter of two days, I went from doing nothing to going full throttle. This was by no means easy however. Although I had regained full feeling in my left arm and hand, I was not at full strength on that side of my body. Carrying a tray of food was an interesting challenge. I'm happy to say I never actually dropped one of them, but there were a couple of close calls. Before my surgery, I was unable to drive. Therefore, if my daughter missed the bus in the morning, my son had to take her. Now that he was incapacitated it was up to me. I hadn't driven in quite a while and still was not anxious to get behind the wheel. It's amazing how heavy a car door can be after you've gone such a long period of time without having to open or close one. Actually, my left arm was still so weak that I couldn't pull the door closed after getting into the driver's seat. I had to reach across my body and close the door with my right hand. There was not enough strength in the left to do it. Needless to say, I was praying she wouldn't miss the bus anytime soon!

Even though this was not the best time of his life, or mine for that matter, it seemed we were growing in our parent/child relationship. Finally, after ten years of ups and downs, on and off, we had found our comfort zone, as a family. It seemed the trials and challenges had served to strengthen our bond and I was now looking forward to more good times than bad. We talked a lot more, since we were both stuck in the house all day. Some days he had visitors come see him and that made his day. It would make me happy to see him in high spirits.

Once I went back to work, I started to feel things shifting backwards in our relationship. It was a familiar feeling, so I knew it almost instantaneously even though there were only one or two small things said, done, or not done. Things were headed south and I could tell.

When the time came that I needed help with something and he made a conscientious decision not to help me, I was hurt. I was disappointed. I was stunned. I am not the type of person who does something for someone with the expectation of receiving anything back. However, I am the type of person who believes family should help family. If I had shown him nothing else over the years, I thought for sure I had shown him that. What I asked for did not require money or any of his other tangible resources. I asked for a few minutes of his time to do something I was physically unable to do. He could have, but he chose not to. For all that I had poured into this young man over the years, it was difficult for me to accept what was happening. "Here we go again", I thought. I actually believed we had made permanent, positive strides.

When the time came to discuss the matter, it did not go well…at all. I may have been speaking with the person I saw as my son, but he was not a fifteen year old boy. He was a thirty year old, grown man who I had done nothing but endeavor to help from the day we met. I didn't feel there was any valid reason I should accept the disrespect I was receiving during the discussion. No mother should be subjected to that level of disrespect from their child, natural born or otherwise.

Our children can cross the line and he certainly did that day. The hurt and disappointment I felt, turned to anger. I was angry that I had been so giving, had made major sacrifices for him, and yet was being treated like I was someone who was out to get him. It was crazy! This was the worst of the 'bad times' we had ever experienced. As much as it pained me, I let him know he had to leave my home...right then. His parting words to me were the most unkind (and profane) anyone has ever spoken to me.

When he left, I knew I was still angry. Even if I had asked God what was going on in this matter, I would not have been able to hear from Him because I was too distracted by emotions (anger, hurt, confusion, disappointment, frustration, betrayal). My heart felt irreparably broken. To be quite frank, I wasn't ready to ask God anything at that point. I wasn't seeking answers. I was too hurt and angry to do that. As the days and weeks passed, I did begin to seek God for an answer. "Lord, this is the worst of the worst. What do you want me to do?" No matter how long I waited, there was no answer. In times past, when things like this (but never as bad as this) happened, I would hear the Lord quite clearly. He would tell me things like "continue on", "show him what family is about," "take him back," "he doesn't know." This time was different. The Lord was absolutely silent. In addition to the silence, which was new, I recognized a new feeling within me. My spirit was at peace.

On several occasions previously, after a falling out, I would have a yearning in my spirit to do something to fix the situation because that's my personality. I'm a problem solver by nature, so when I see one I think it rests solely on my shoulders to fix. This time was different. Even after the emotions subsided and I was able to think clearly, I realized I did not have the urge to fix it this time. I began to understand that the peace I felt and the silence was God's way of telling me I had done all I could. I love my son and always endeavored to show him that in words and in deeds.

There was no message from the Lord this time directing me to try again or show him what family is about. The silence meant I had done my part. I had tried and I showed him all I knew. I gave it all that I had. I believe there are times when we have to let our kids go long enough for them to realize some things on their own.

"Train up a child in the way he should go; and when he is old, he will not depart from it." Proverbs 22:6 I did the best I knew how to do. Maybe one day the tide will turn and a positive, healthy relationship can be salvaged. As a mother, that is my prayer.

Way Maker

The bills were mounting. Three visits to the emergency room, a two-day stay in the hospital, visits to the surgeon's office, diagnostic testing, and the surgery itself all resulted in a mountain of bills that came in the mail.My regular expenses (mortgage, car payment, insurance, utilities, etc.) were being paid with no problem. I had been employed with the same organization for nineteen years and had enough sick time accumulated, so there was no loss of income as a result of being out of work for an extended period of time. The pile of medical bills actually stood six inches high! Paying them was going to be another story. I did have health insurance and was grateful for it. I imagine the only thing worse than dealing with a health crisis is wondering how to pay for it. At least with my insurance I would not be responsible for the full cost of everything. Judging by the depth of the stack of bills I had received, it appeared likely that my small portion of the financial responsibility was still going to be more than I was prepared to pay.

One thing I began to understand after the surgery was stress was a no-no. I couldn't afford to stress over the bills, or anything else for that matter. My health needed to finally come first. I couldn't afford to be stressed because it would hinder my physical recovery. More importantly, since the time I accepted Christ, I've seen Him on more than one occasion make a way when I didn't see any possibilities of a solution. The bills would get paid, of that I was confident. It just wasn't time yet to know how.

So, I developed a strategy. Please pay close attention because I want you to catch this. My strategy was to do nothing. I literally let them pile up. This wasn't just for a week or two. I let them pile up for months because I knew it would take a while to receive all final invoices from the various service providers. Mid-January 2013 was the onset of the condition and the surgery was not until the end of February. It would be a while before all of the doctors, hospitals, imaging centers, anesthesiologists, etc. got their billing together, to submit to my insurance company, and then be able to send me invoices of balances due. I didn't want to open them as they came in the mail one at a time because I didn't want to give myself the opportunity to stress over them, or question how they were going to get paid. Amazingly, I was comfortable with this approach. This was so contrary to how I was raised. When a bill comes in the mail you pay it. That's how my parents lived. That was the example I saw growing up and that's what I typically did as well. This situation was different, altogether. I can honestly say I felt led by the Spirit to leave them alone.

One day my Mom asked about the status of my medical bills. Nonchalantly, I let her know of my 'strategy'. I could tell she did not agree and was concerned with my approach. She didn't question me about it which I appreciated. That too, would have turned into stress for me. I knew full well she thought I was doing the wrong thing. Typically, she would say what she felt and let the chips fall where they may. Now that I'm an adult and a mother, I'm not sure she is any different than most moms.

Mothers want what is best for their kids. We try to lead and guide our children the best we know how, which often times means speaking our opinion. But this time, she didn't and I attributed that to her understanding as well that I could not afford to feel stress. I was comfortable with how I chose to handle the bills and she let it be.

One evening after work in mid-April 2013, I knew the time had come to go through the mound of bills. How did I know? To tell you the truth, I'm not exactly sure. I just felt ready in my spirit to handle whatever was inside each of the envelopes. It was finally time to grab the pile, sort them by payee, sort by date received, open them, and see the financial damage. Even with health insurance there were co-pays and deductibles I was responsible for paying.

I went to the kitchen, got a plastic trash bag, sat in my recliner, and opened every envelope one by one. When I could identify duplicates, I ripped them up and put them in the bag. In some cases, I had received triplicates and more. Virtually all of them were past due. Many of them were severely overdue.

Once the pile dwindled down, I had a good picture of my financial responsibility. My first thought was,"Okay, Lord, you know I don't have money to pay for all of this. I'm going to need you to make a way." There was no stress, panic, or anxiety about it; no tearful pleading. Somehow, that provided confirmation for me that my strategy was in-line with what He wanted me to do. It didn't make people-sense to have sat on those bills for so long, but it seemed to make perfect God-sense.

Some of the bills were quite manageable. Surprisingly enough, I still didn't feel led to pay them off. At this point, even I was becoming a little curious at the strategy that had been placed in my spirit.

Curious or not, I obeyed what I felt. I let the condensed pile of mail sit a little longer without paying a single one of them. This makes me sound quite irresponsible and I realize that. It's very important for me to be transparent about this in order to show how God had His hand in everything from the beginning to the end.

When you let the Holy Spirit guide you, you'll find yourself doing things that don't make sense to your natural mind. That's where faith is found! The first week of May 2013 our company held a benefits meeting. I had already selected my benefits for that year and we were just about at the half-way point of the year. I couldn't understand the purpose of bringing in the people from the dental and medical insurance companies when we couldn't make changes to the plan we had previously selected. Since the meeting was not mandatory, I decided that I wasn't going. I didn't need to. I thought it would be a waste of my time. If we were able to make changes, that would have been worth me going. During open enrollment several months earlier, we were given an opportunity to elect short-term disability coverage. It had never been offered to us before and I strongly considered getting the additional insurance. Opting for this coverage would have resulted in more money taken out of my check each pay period. Because of all the other deductions that were being taken out of my paycheck each month (cost of health insurance, income taxes, savings/investment plans), I wasn't sure I could spare anything more.

So, I talked myself out of getting it for that reason alone. What a mistake! Had I signed up for short term disability, I would have had the money needed to pay the medical bills.

When I look back and reflect on the opportunity I had to select the coverage and remember how strongly I considered it, I wonder if that was another opportunity the Holy Spirit was giving me to heed His gentle nudging. I believe that is the case. In nineteen years, my company had not made this coverage available to us. The first year it was made available, I contemplated getting it but did not. A few short months later, I would have benefitted greatly from having it!

I didn't realize the gentle nudging for what it was. Although, I was now disappointed in myself for having been spiritually disobedient, I still believed it would work out alright... somehow.

The morning of the benefits meeting, it seemed I had a change of heart and decided to attend. Actually, it felt more like I was supposed to go to the meeting. Thankfully, no RSVP had been required, enabling me to walk in just as it was about to begin.

While the representatives talked, I can't say I felt being there was worth my time. It seemed like it was a repeat of the information presented to us during open enrollment back in the Fall. So again, what was the point? They didn't even have refreshments there to make it worth the time spent sitting and listening! Then....at the very end, I heard something I had not known before and my interest was piqued. The representative from the healthcare company explained she is dedicated solely to the employees of our organization. Although she works for the healthcare provider, her job was to assist our employees only. She went on to say, if we ever have a question about our medical claims, we should feel free to talk with her. This interested me, but I still wasn't sure why. I knew I had incurred the charges outlined in the stack of medical bills, so I figured I would surely be responsible for paying them. The doctors, hospitals, and others had already submitted their bills to the insurance provider. The insurance provider had already reviewed them and paid the portions they were responsible for based on our company's plan. The bills I received were the final determination of my financial obligation... right? As I mentioned before He will make a way when we can't see a way. Well, He was about to do it again!

After the meeting, I spoke with the healthcare representative privately. I briefly explained what I had gone through in January and February. I told her I had just weeded through the mound of bills and was prepared to start chipping away at them the best I could. Some would certainly have to be set up as payment plans, others I could pay in full at any time. She asked if I wanted her to take a look at them before I made any payments. If there was even a chance she could find an error or an adjustment that would work in my favor, I was willing to try.

Coincidentally, or was it a coincidence? Life has taught me there are no coincidences in Christ. I had all of the bills with me that day at work. They were downstairs in my office. When the meeting was over, I made a copy and faxed them to her office for review. She promptly acknowledged receiving the information and let me know she would get back to me within three days. Honestly, I don't know if I was expecting anything to come from this or not. Over the next few days I posed every possibility in my head while waiting to hear back from her. "Ms. Wilson, I've reviewed every bill and they are all correct. Feel free to proceed with paying the providers." Or, would she call me and say, "Ms. Wilson, we have found all invoices to be correct except the one for $11. That was our error and we will pay that one. Feel free to proceed with paying the other providers." I wasn't sure what she would call and say, and there was a part of me that wondered if she would call at all.

True to her word, she called me on the third business day. That alone impressed me. When she called, she wanted to know if I had the bills with me. I didn't have the actual ones, but I did still have the copies that had been faxed to her a few days earlier. Once I had them in-hand, we went through them one at a time. She began speaking. "This one was coded incorrectly. We will take care of paying that one. You can disregard it." "This one they did not recognize as being affiliated with the day of your surgery. We will pay that one.

You can disregard it also." By the time we went through each bill I thought I was responsible for paying, she let me know my actual financial responsibility was exactly HALF the dollar amount of what the bills indicated! What in the world had the Lord just done!!! This is how He made a way. He cut in half the amount I was to pay! To further show His awesomeness, there was one bill from my surgeon whitch was not only incorrect, but it turned out the surgeon owed me money! Now that's God! To go from owing thousands of dollars to the amount being reduced to literally half the amount, and then getting a little money back on top of that was incredible! It was amazing how God was blessing me.

My response to her on the phone was a borderline scream,"Praise the Lord and thank you Jesus!" I honestly did not care if it was the politically correct thing to say or not. God had just blessed me in a significant way and I HAD to give Him the glory and honor for doing it at that very moment.

The lesson that was reinforced for me that day was to continue trusting God despite the way things look. Although it was a foreign concept for me to let bills go unpaid, I did it because I knew He told me to wait. I pray no one reads this and misinterprets what I'm saying and stops paying their bills. That is not the point at all. The point is to listen and yield to the gentle guidance of the Holy Spirit in your own life. He won't steer your wrong.

Had I done what made people-sense I would have paid those bills needlessly, to the tune of several thousand dollars. The various providers would have accepted my payments because their computerized billing systems said I owed it. Having all of the bills re-reviewed by the insurance company is where God was able to go to work. There was an error here, an error there, and some oversights He was able to bring to light. It took faith to trust Him in this way, but I'm glad I did!

I was elated over this good news! I had to call and tell someone. The first person who came to mind was my Bishop's wife. When she answered the phone, I could hardly compose myself enough to talk. I was so excited to tell her how God had just blessed me! She had the reaction I knew she would; she praised Him too! When I began going to their church more than ten years earlier, we formed a special relationship. It was as if she took me under her wing for a while and nurtured me, almost like a daughter. This allowed me to be a bit closer to her than what may be considered typical for a church member. I've been at the hospital with her at times when she was sick, but still strong in her faith. One of the greatest testimonies I've ever heard came from her. She has told this publically so I'm sure she won't mind me sharing it here with you. There was a time when, because of the severity of a health issue, she did not know who she was. The amazing thing was she never forgot WHOSE she was! She may not have been able to remember her name, but she remembered to pray! She is the greatest woman of faith this side of Heaven, not 'one of the greatest'. I sincerely mean THE greatest woman of faith I've ever known personally. I have learned so much from her in regards to faith. She doesn't teach faith by telling you about it, she teaches it by showing you her faith in action. This is one of the things I love most about her, so I have observed her closely over the years in situations others would buckle in. Her actions line up with her words when the time comes to stand on nothing more than sheer faith.

I was blessed to give remarks one year at a program held in her honor. I remember saying she is who women like me aspire to be, in Christ, as we move through our spiritual journey. What I said was true then, and still is. Her life has not been easy, far from it, but her faith is rock solid. She lives by it. She has held to it during times of physical struggles, financial challenges, and family issues. Her faith is what she goes to first in tough times. You don't see her down and you don't hear her speak negatively. It is not just a public face she puts on when she thinks people are looking, it is the foundation of who she is: a woman of unwavering faith.

Although there was a brief period in time when she didn't know who she was, she knew whose she was and that's how we have to be also. We have to know and believe, despite all we're going through, He is with us and for us and the temporary, yet painful situations and circumstances will pass. We may not even recognize ourselves anymore in the midst of all that's going on, but we have to know who we belong to and know everything really will be alright!

I have no doubt had the Lord not placed her in my life years ago, I would not have been able to put my own faith into action throughout my health ordeal and recovery. For Him and her, I am eternally grateful.

He had done it yet, again. He gave me what I needed when I needed it. Why the Lord loves me so I truly will never know, but I do know I am very thankful He does. The love He has for me is as deep as the love He has for you. The only thing He wants is for us to trust Him enough to give Him an opportunity to show us His love. I'm glad I gave Him the opportunity with that stack of bills!

Parking Space Faith

For years now, whenever I go to the mall or a large shopping center, I always ask God to bless me with a good parking space. Despite the common stereotype of women, I do not like shopping. It is more of a chore for me than something I enjoy. Seriously, I rank shopping up there with scrubbing the kitchen floor. I see it as something I have to do and I don't look forward to it at all. Having to search for a parking space only adds to the disdain I have for the overall experience of shopping.

When I first started doing this my daughter was pretty young. She has grown up hearing me ask the Lord for parking space favor as long as she can remember. To her, it's the normal thing to do. We actually laugh about it sometimes because I can get pretty animated when I get a really good spot! It almost makes the madness of shopping tolerable if I can park close to the entrance.

I would venture to say He grants my request about 95% of the time. When He does, I'm thankful. Sometimes, I even chuckle because I think it's sweet He does it for me. The times I have to park a bit further out are so few and far between I can't be mad or upset. I thank Him nonetheless because there's probably a very good reason for it. It could be I need the exercise anyway to walk off a large meal I had just eaten – who knows. I look for the positive even when a premium parking space isn't provided for me.

When I think about the ninety-five percent 'success rate', I often wonder why He does it so frequently. I can't think of any other prayer I pray that has gotten the same results. (Wouldn't it be nice, especially on payday: "Lord, please let there be extra money in my check." If only there was a ninety- five percent success rate with that one!) Something hit my spirit concerning this one day. Could it be that it's too easy for Him? After all, it is just a parking space we're talking about here! I imagine He too often wonders something. Maybe He wonders when I'll believe Him for something bigger. Sure, I have parking space faith, but is that the extent of my faith in Him. Do I think He is incapable of anything more than that? I wonder if sometimes He is actually a little disappointed I have not asked for more. I imagine Him looking down from Heaven, while I park my car in the premium spot He provided, and saying, "Daughter, is this all you have faith to believe in me for…a mere parking space?"

Well let me tell you, there was a time when I did dare to believe Him for more than up-front parking and He didn't let me down. I remember the time He blessed me with a nice vehicle to go in those premium parking spaces. He didn't just make a way for me to purchase one. That would be blessing enough if that had been the case. I didn't purchase one, I was given one! How it happened is the best part.

Several years ago, I had been having major car problems. I loved my car but it was really starting to cause me some stress. I had purchased it used and after a couple years things began going wrong with it, major things. It was a Mercedes Benz, and most things on it or in it were expensive to repair or replace. I knew I needed to get rid of it but didn't know how I would be able to. The timing was not good, as if it ever is when these things happen. Although I was a bit frustrated by the situation I didn't blow a gasket (pun intended). I assumed I would eventually figure out what to do.

One afternoon I was out with a friend. While riding down the road, we were having a basic conversation which was totally unrelated to my car dilemma. Out of nowhere, I remember saying, "Someone's going to give me a car". It was such an out of place statement but I remember saying it with so much conviction. Two thoughts came to me immediately, "Where did that come from?" and "I don't know anyone who has the ability to give me a car."

Neither of my two thoughts (doubts) was verbally expressed, only the bold declaration that someone would bless me with a car. When I said it, my friend replied with "I believe you". He agreed with me! This was one of those I remember where I was when it happened moments. To this day, I remember exactly where we were on the road when this was said and agreed upon. The whole thing was perplexing because I don't know what made me say that, except for the fact that I had a need for another vehicle. Other than my parents, when I was a teenager, no one had ever given me a car. Why would they? We work for what we need and want, right?

Nonetheless, once it was said, I decided to stand on it and believe God for it! At that point, the battle began. My natural mind could not compute how this could or would happen, yet my spirit told me to continue believing it could and would happen. Even though I never had a conscious thought that someone would do this, it felt right when I said it. Apparently my spirit was in agreement with the statement. I wonder if you've ever experienced something similar. You claimed something and weren't even sure why, but it felt right? Did you stand on it or did you dismiss it as foolishness?

As crazy as it was, I did not dismiss it as foolishness. I actually found myself wondering who it would be that would bless me in such a way. I wondered when it would happen. I even wondered what kind of car I'd be given. As strange as all of that may sound, the amazing part is I didn't have to wonder for long. Within two months of making that statement I was given a fully loaded BMW X5. Honestly speaking, it may have been less than two months but since I can't recall the specific timeline, I rounded it up.

My brother had gone overseas to work in Afghanistan. He had already been gone for a few months when I started having car troubles. The job he accepted required him to be gone for two years. When he left the states he put his two cars in storage at our parent's houses. Both of our parents had vehicles so they were not driving his. His were under car covers, just sitting there.

Even though my brother knew of the problems I was having with the Mercedes, it never crossed my mind he would offer me one of his vehicles, but he did. He suggested I sell my car and drive his X5. He actually made me feel as if I was doing him a favor, telling me it would not be good for it to sit idle for such a long period of time. Well, alrighty then! As long as I was doing him a favor, I graciously accepted his offer. That's what a good sister would do, right? Seriously, I did not see that coming...at all. It never crossed my mind he would make such an offer. I was beyond speechless.

I had been frustrated with the car predicament, but it was causing more than just a little angst. My daughter and I had been left stranded on the side of the road once while on an out of town trip during her Spring Break. Another time, the car broke down on a dangerous stretch of the interstate. Those were matters of safety I could not ignore. Each time I had to sink money into it for repairs, it hit me hard financially. Keep in mind I was still making a car payment on it, as well. The car put me in the hole financially. The offer my brother made was a two-fold blessing. It allowed me to get rid of the money pit while driving the X5 which was already paid for. This gave me a chance to get my head above water, financially speaking.

What do you think would have happened had I not allowed those words to come out of my mouth? What would have happened had I spoken them but then pronounced doubt afterwards? What if I would have yielded to my natural mind and began talking myself out of the blessing God was offering me? What if I had said, "That was silly, why did I say that? No one's going to just give me a car." I may have canceled the blessing God had coming my way. If I had, it likely may not have been the first time. We don't recognize the power of our own words. We put disclaimers out there to protect ourselves. We don't want to be disappointed if we don't receive what we've asked for. We have to understand God longs to be good to us (*Isaiah 30:18 Therefore the Lord will wait, that He may be gracious to you;*

and therefore He will be exalted, that He may have mercy on you. For the Lord is a God of justice; blessed are all those who wait for Him), to give us the desires of our hearts. But He needs us to stretch our faith in order to receive them. I don't know about you, but I want everything God has for me. Parking space faith may be a good starting point but that's not where it has to end. Frankly, as children of the most-high God, I don't think that's where it is supposed to end.

Where does your faith need to be stretched a little to receive blessings of a higher level? Are you good at praying for others to be blessed but find it hard to do the same for yourself? What is it you are believing God for in your own life? Please call it! Call it from the spiritual realm into the natural. You may not need a reliable car like I did at that time, but if you're living (which you are because you're reading this book), you have a need of some sort. Maybe yours is for peace in a turbulent relationship, or for finances, or for healing. Maybe it's for a mate that will love you for you, or for your children to be saved. Maybe it's for a promotion you know you deserve and have worked hard for. It could be you're seeking wisdom so you feel better equipped to make life decisions. I don't know what your need is but you and God do.

He wants you to ask for it, believe He will do it, and then watch Him bring it to pass. When He does, please be sure to give Him the honor and the glory because that's what He deserves.

When I took possession of the X5, I went through the required process of registering it to get license plates. I hadn't had personalized plates since I was in college and was tempted to get something special for this occasion. I tried to think of something that would be an indication to other drivers that God had blessed me. It wasn't going to be for purposes of showing off, not by any means. The purpose was to show my thanks for how God had blessed me. I decided it wasn't really necessary. I knew I had been blessed and every time I got in the BMW, I thanked the Lord. What my brother had done for me was huge, so I thanked him repeatedly as well. Although he has never said this, I wonder if he questioned himself as to why he was giving me his vehicle. "Give her my truck? No, I don't think so. She's grown. She's self-sufficient, she'll work it out." Even if he had made the offer and then rescinded it at the last minute, I wouldn't have been mad. I didn't expect him to do this for me.

While sitting at the DMV completing all of the necessary paperwork, the clerk reached in her desk drawer and pulled out an envelope that looked to be the same size as license plates. I assumed that's what it was and I was correct. When all of the documents had been properly completed, she opened the envelope, pulled out the plate, and I saw '4ME'. Whatever came after the dash, I don't remember. Even after driving the vehicle those two years, I don't remember. It was so significant to me that it began with "4ME". Tell me that's not God! He personalized the plates for me in His own way, and all at the same time was letting me know He did it (worked out my car problems) 4ME!

Once the plate had been put on, I got in and started driving. I had nowhere specific to go but I needed some communion time with the Lord. I drove, I cried, I praised, and I thanked Him. I was able to keep the vehicle for two years and it gave me the financial breathing room I needed. When my brother returned from Afghanistan, he was in no hurry to get the X5 back because he had another vehicle. However, the two-year reprieve allowed me time to get my finances together and I was ready to purchase a car of my own. Once the purchase was done, I made plans to meet up him to return the SUV. For weeks after that, each time I got in my new car, I thought of my brother. I thought of how much better off I was because of the kindness he extended to me. I remember calling him a couple of times after returning the BMW to say thank you, yet again, because it meant so much to me.

Faith is like a muscle, the more you use it the stronger it gets. Flex your spiritual muscles and watch God work on your behalf. Whatever He has done for me, He can do for you. He just asks us to have faith *(Mark 11:22 "And Jesus answering said unto them, have faith in God.")*. No matter what things look like in the natural, let your faith in God sustain you because He is in ALL things…great and small!

CHAPTER

9 | No More

July 6, 2013 is a day I will not soon forget, but not for any good reason or pleasant memory. One of my co-workers of nineteen years was brutally attacked by a stranger. He was beaten within a breath of his life. Everyone at work was mortified. He was one of the nicest and happiest people I've ever known. How someone could do that to him was something I could not fathom. Why would anyone do this? Who would do this? It was hard to comprehend.

He spent the next two months in ICU fighting for his life. Despite the severity of his injuries we all held out hope for a miracle, but on September 12, 2013 he passed away.

In the nineteen years we worked together, I can't ever remember seeing him lose his cool. There was nothing I ever needed that he didn't do, gladly. Some of our clients were quite demanding. Worse than that, many were very indecisive. As a result, he and the other electricians would have to set power, pick it up, move it, and possibly do it over again thirty minutes later. Still, he never complained. I, on the other hand, would feel bad for having them do double work. Of course, I tried to avoid it by giving our clients other viable options but sometimes there was no choice. When approaching him to ask that he relocate the electrical connections yet again, I felt bad that my powers of persuasion with the client weren't strong enough to convince them to leave it as-is. It didn't seem to matter, he never minded. He would always say, "Don't worry about it Shawn-Ta. That's what I'm here for." Now, there are some people who say that, but at the same time, their facial expressions may be saying something different, something more along the lines of, "I can't believe I have to do this again!" This was never in his spirit. His words and his facial expressions always lined up. He said he was glad to do it, glad to help, and he was. The only time I heard him complain about anything was when it was cold outside. Living in Florida, we don't get much cold weather. When the cold weather came he absolutely hated it. He was a thin man in stature and he detested the cold. As he walked around the building on those chilly days, his hands would be in his pockets and his jacket zipped up to his neck. Having grown up in Virginia, I always missed the change of seasons but he did not. When I would see him on one of those Florida-frigid fifty degree days I would joke with him about how much I knew he was enjoying it. He would always say, "This is why I left New York!" My co-worker was simply and uniquely a happy man. The main source of his happiness was his daughter. She was his world. Even on a cold weather day, you could still get a mile-wide smile out of him just by mentioning her name. As co-workers go they just don't get any better than him.

One Sunday morning I was scheduled to be at work at 7am. On the way, I got a flat tire. I called ahead to say I would be late. He was on duty so I spoke with him. When I told him of my situation he didn't hesitate for even a moment before offering to come and assist me on the side of the road. Someone was already on their way to help me, but I appreciated his sincere offer nonetheless. That's the type of person he was, always there to help in any way he could.

He was such a huge presence in our workplace. The first few weeks after his death, I still expected to see him come around a corner as I made rounds in the facility. Sometimes just the sight of an extension cord on the floor would send me into tears. I just couldn't believe he was gone. His death hit me so much harder than I would have ever expected, and it caught me way off guard. From the time I was seven years old I have dealt with the painful realities of death, especially tragic ones. When you have an uncle drown, an uncle die in a house fire (caused by an intentional bombing), a grandfather die in a car accident, a cousin get shot, and another cousin die suddenly, a short time after having her baby, you pretty much feel as if you've gotten accustomed to the sting of death. When my co-worker died, I realized that was not true, at all.

For a few months after his passing, I would often wonder why his death seemed to rock me to the core. Yes, he was a wonderful person. Yes, I knew I would miss him and his funny personality at work. Yes, I knew I would miss exchanging stories with him about our daughters. This was all true, but still, the question remained. Why did I feel so totally devastated? Was it because of the sheer brutality of his attack? No person, let alone him, deserved what happened to him. Was it the senselessness of what happened to him that added to the depth of my grief? All I knew was at this point, I could take no more of what 2013 was dishing out to me in such generous portions. Nine months into the calendar year of 2013 and I had already experienced enough anguish, grief, loss, and pain (physical and emotional) to last the next ten years!

Sadly, no matter how bad the year had gone thus far, nothing could have prepared me for what would occur in October. In just a matter of a second, a life ended and my life would never again be the same. I find clichés so annoying, yet the sad fact of the matter is there is so much truth behind that one in particular. My life has not been the same since October 2013.

One Friday afternoon in October, I set out to find the local newspaper to see what would be happening in town over the weekend. Most Saturdays I look forward to sleeping in and then doing whatever my mood dictates after that. On this day, however, I felt like making a plan for Saturday instead of choosing an activity, spur of the moment. I left the office and headed outside to where I thought there was a newspaper machine. There wasn't one there but a co-worker was finished with his so he gave it to me. With the newspaper in hand, I went back to my office to scan the pages. There is no shortage of things to do in our area so I knew the choices would be many. For eighteen years my work schedule was erratic and included nights, holidays, weekends, and long stretches of days in a row without a day off. Right around this time frame, I was blessed with a new position. My new schedule was Monday through Friday only. I was bound and determined to make up for all the weekends I spent at work by finding something fun to do every weekend. Managing events is fascinating and fun, but demanding....especially on your home and personal life.

As I flipped through the pages of the paper nothing much caught my eye. Not yet discouraged, I kept looking, turning the pages, and scanning the headlines. Flipping to the next page, I noticed an article about an accident that had taken place downtown two nights prior. This obviously wasn't what I was searching for, but there was something in me that made me stop and read it. The quest for weekend activities was abruptly and permanently suspended when I read "64 year old Bernadine Frances Davis Smith of Riverview died at the scene". I had to stop and re-read it. I did and then had to do it one more time. "I know this is not my Ms. Bernie", I thought. "Okay, it can't be her. She isn't sixty-four like the article indicated, she just turned sixty-five in August," I reasoned with myself.

I reached for my desk calendar and pulled it closer to me. So I don't forget birthdays of people close to me, I write them on my calendar every year. I turned back the pages until I got to August 2nd. Written on that day was "Ms. Bernie (64)". I didn't care what my calendar said, it still didn't matter. This article surely was not telling me my Ms. Bernie was gone. This was going to turn out to be a really strange coincidence of the name, age, and town. That's what I was trying to tell myself, but the feeling I was getting in the pit of my stomach was telling me something altogether different. Have you ever had that burning feeling on the inside when you know something terrible has happened? Everything in me felt like it was on fire!

I knew if I called her cell phone I would be able to dismiss this whole thing. She and I would then pray on the phone for the woman who died two nights earlier. We would then talk about our weekend plans, and determine if we would see one another Sunday after our respective church services. Whenever I cooked on Sundays I would invite her over. She stayed so busy she didn't cook much for herself. I thoroughly enjoyed providing meals for her when I could because she genuinely appreciated it. Depending upon how much time she had, she would either come in, sit, eat her food, or she would come in, visit for a while and then take her food to go. Either way was fine with me. I just enjoyed her company and she enjoyed my food. Some of her favorite meals were the fried fish, macaroni and cheese, and greens, stewed turkey wings with rice and corn muffins, roast beef, mashed potatoes, and cabbage. Oh, and the chicken salad.

Over the past three years she had become part of my family. A family visit with her was always a blessing. Eager to settle the sick feeling I had in my stomach which was now creating a huge knot in my throat, I picked up my cell phone to call her. I pulled up the recent calls log, quickly found her name, and hit the little green icon to initiate the call. To my surprise, it went to her voicemail on the first ring.

Had this been morning time, I wouldn't have thought twice about that. Ms. Bernie turns her phone off when she goes to bed and turns it back on when she is up and moving for the day. This was late in the afternoon. Why would her phone be going straight to voicemail? "No worries", I thought. "I'll just leave a message". The only thing I could bring myself to say was, "Hey Ms. Bernie, it's me. Give me a call as soon as you can. It's important."

Still, even still, I was trying my best to remain calm and rationalize everything that was telling me what I did not want to accept. I remember thinking, "Maybe she is in a meeting at the church so she sent the call to voicemail. I'll just text her. She'll be able to reply to a text even if she is in a meeting". Without hesitation, I sent her a quick message and said, "Please call, It's important." I waited for a response for what felt like an hour. In reality, it was probably only twenty seconds. I didn't know what to do after that. It wasn't feeling right…something just wasn't right. What could I do next? I needed to reach her.

Although she had been fully integrated into my entire life, I didn't know her family. I had met her best friend once but I didn't have contact information for her. I had been introduced to a daughter-in-law once when I stopped by at Thanksgiving to give Ms. Bernie a loaf of pumpkin bread. I didn't have any way of contacting her, either. Well, there were the sons. I had heard about all of the sons to the point where I felt I knew them. Sadly, I had not met any of them. From time to time, Ms. Bernie and I would talk about how I needed to meet her family. She told me they, and her friends, knew of me because she often talked about me to them. Yet, I didn't know them. I had no one else to call. The short article did reference a report written by the police department, so I called them. Unfortunately, they weren't able to give me any more information than what was in the article. By now, all calmness was gone. I was in full blown panic mode. "I CANNOT LOSE MY MS. BERNIE" kept going through my mind. That would be entirely too much to bear. As panic mode set in, I shared with my office mate what was going on. At the same time, I called a friend to tell her what I had just found in the newspaper. As I was on the phone with my friend, my office mate said he found another article online with a few additional details. I asked my friend to hold on so I could hear what he was telling me. I didn't actually put the call on hold, just kind of held on to the receiver. My office mate asked if I knew Ms. Bernie's address. I did know it, but at that moment there was no way I was thinking clearly enough to recall it. What I could remember though was her address was really easy. I told him if he read it to me I would know right away if it was hers. When he said the street number it didn't register. But when he said "Marc Drive", I lost it! Oh my God, it was Ms. Bernie! Please Lord, not my friend, my spiritual mentor. This just could not be happening! There simply are no words to explain what I went through after that. The fact that my friend was holding on the phone and extremely concerned wasn't enough to make me pull it together. I couldn't do anything but fall to pieces. That's literally how I felt on the inside. My heart felt like it was detaching from my very soul, slowly and quite painfully. I felt as if I was coming apart at the seams and life was being sucked out of me. I struggled to breathe.

Here I was, preparing to fully enjoy the weekend but instead I had just read in the newspaper that this lady, whom I loved dearly and admired greatly, was killed two nights prior and I didn't even know. It was too much; too much to process, too much to handle, too much to accept. Just too much!

It's amazing how many thoughts can go through your mind at lightning speed at times like this. I thought of how we had spoken so often about going to the Holy Land Experience in Orlando together but we had not yet done so. Now we would never have the opportunity. I thought about how it had been a few days since we last spoke and I was feeling regret about that already. Thoughts of Sunday dinners without her started running through my mind and I began to wonder how in the world I was going to make it without her now. She had become so much to me in such a short span of three years. Those three years may as well have been thirty because of the closeness we shared.

Needless to say, there wasn't anything about that weekend I enjoyed. Did I really have to go home and tell my daughter Ms. Bernie was gone? I just about choked on the words as they came out of my mouth. I didn't want to say them because I still didn't want to accept it was real.

By now, the full weight of everything I had endured that year was bearing down on me. I couldn't take it anymore. I had cried out and asked God why and what. Why was all of this happening in my world in such a condensed period of time? What did I do to deserve such continual, intense suffering? Those questions may seem selfish or self-centered but I really needed to know! People I cared about were being taken from me and walking away from me almost as if it were punishment. I needed to know if there was something I was supposed to be doing differently or better. If there was, I had to know and I had to know now! I CAN'T TAKE ANYTHING ELSE! Not one more thing could I handle, emotionally, psychologically, or physically.

Sitting in my office that Friday afternoon, surrounded by concerned co-workers, between gasps and sobs, those words were repeated over and over again. I said them, I screamed them, I cried them, my heart declared them and my insides felt them. It was my way of telling the Lord that I really did not think I could handle one more thing in this calendar year. I begged Him, "Please Lord, just let me ride it out now. Enough is enough". I may not have actually verbalized the statement but my heart certainly cried it and I was praying God heard me by way of my tears. It was only October and 2013 had brought so much pain, agony, sadness, and sorrow my way. All I wanted was to let the last two months of 2013 pass by. I wanted to exist but I didn't want to engage in life for the next two months. I wanted to be left alone to heal. There were some moments I literally had to will myself to breathe. I was that exhausted and beat down.

"Now faith is the substance of things hoped for, the evidence of things not seen" (Hebrews 11:1). When Ms. Bernie passed, I felt that was the final straw. There had just been too much. There was no peace in sight but my faith allowed me to believe it would come. It was an incredibly tough time to get through but I knew I couldn't give up, no matter how much I was hurting. I tried hard to keep the faith and believe I would bounce back from this most devastating turn of events. I hoped everything would level out even though I couldn't see any indication that it was. Regardless, I needed to believe it would. I believed God for grace so that I could endure until this season of turmoil, sadness, and heartbreak in my life was over.

God bless my co-workers. They were super supportive. They seemed to realize the only thing they could do to help me in that moment was to love me through it, and they did. Grief is a process that has to begin in order to end. They saw me through the very initial stage with hugs, tissues, and softly spoken kind words. Eventually I was able to leave work and feel that I could drive home safely. I had to promise them if a wave of emotion came over me in the car, I would pull to the side of the road and work through it. I told them I would and I meant it.

Ms. Bernie's home-going service would have made her happy. Scratch that, it made her happy! There is no doubt within me she looked down from above with joy. The service was a celebration for sure. She loved her church, her church family, and they loved her right back. She was a tireless servant. She deemed it a true honor to serve within her church, and she participated in all she could.

I'm sure it pleased her greatly that the Bishop of her church presided over the service himself. She meant so much to so many people. Even the Bishop had to admit when he heard the news of her passing he briefly asked the Lord, "Why?" That was a powerful admission. First, it let everyone know just how much Ms. Bernie was loved and respected by everyone, including him. Secondly, it reminded us all that even a person of his position is human. She touched his life as deeply as she touched ours and he too, felt a great sense of loss at her passing. By the way, she did pass, she did not die. *She passed into eternal life (John 5:24)* and I believe that with my whole heart. At that time, she was the first person who I never wondered if they were heaven bound. She surely went to heaven. She exemplified Christ in all she did. I loved and admired that about her. I would often wonder if I would be as adept at handling life the way she did, once I reached her age. It is my prayer that I will be.

One Sunday morning, I heard a preacher on television talk about Stephen who, when he went to heaven, Jesus stood to greet him. I have absolutely no doubt this was the welcome Ms. Bernie received. Her good works on earth were too many to count. That's why she didn't always have time to come in and eat her food at the house. She was always on the move going to help someone. She was happiest that way.

Knowing she went to heaven was comforting. The only other thing that gave me any solace was my confidence in the fact that she knew I loved and appreciated her. We always greeted each other with a hug. When the time came to part ways after our visits or outings together, we didn't leave each other's presence without another hug. When we spoke on the phone, I always told her I loved her at the end of the conversation. Her warm, sincere voice would then say, "I love you too, baby." That's who I was to her, her baby.

It was weeks after her passing before her baby could even cook again on a Sunday. Beyond that, it was months before her baby could think of her and not cry. I can think of her now and smile. I can think of her now and be happy that she is in heaven. I can think of her now and allow her life to continue to inspire me.

CHAPTER 10

Something To Look Forward To

With all that transpired in the year, I really needed something to look forward to. Thanksgiving was on the horizon and I thought quality, family time would be a good break from the craziness that had become my life. A 10-day trip home to Virginia and West Virginia was long overdue. It had been quite a while since I spent a Thanksgiving with my family (mom, dad, brother, aunts, uncle, cousins), and even longer since I had seen some of my friends from high school. The excitement was building and not even the bitterly cold weather they were having in those states deterred me. Actually, it was appealing to me. I wasn't quite sure I was prepared with cold weather clothes and shoes though. A sweater in Florida terms means something completely different than Northern terms. So, I packed in preparation to dress in many layers in order to stay warm enough.

Two days before leaving on my holiday excursion, I apparently came in contact with something I am highly allergic to. Food allergies have plagued me my whole life. Typically, I am very careful and ask lots of questions about food when eating away from home. There have been several close calls over the years, in restaurants and even on an airplane once. It amazes me when I encounter servers who seem to know very little about the food they are serving. I've spoken with servers and restaurant managers who don't seem to understand how incredibly serious food allergies are. The reality is, they can be deadly.

In this particular case, it was cross-contamination. I hadn't actually eaten anything I am allergic to. What I ate simply touched something I'm allergic to. That's how sensitive and severe food allergies can be. The cross-contamination was enough to cause the second worse reaction in my life! In the beginning, it was easy to handle the itchy throat. As a matter of fact, I tried to ride it out and not make a big deal out of it. It's happened once or twice in the past that a reaction hasn't gone full-blown. This would not be one of those times, unfortunately. When I felt my tongue swelling, I went into denial. There was no way, two days before my trip, I was going to the hospital. "It will go away", is what I kept saying to myself, even though life experience had taught me better than that.

By the time I started showing my concern, the people around me were very concerned. Although I had been in denial, they were not. Some of them have been with me at work when it has happened before. They've seen the paramedics have to give me shots of Epinephrine and Benadryl. They know I am supposed to carry an Epi-Pen, but on that day, I did not have one with me. It wouldn't have mattered. By the time I accepted what was happening, I needed much more than an Epi-Pen could provide. Once my throat began closing, I couldn't fight it anymore. I had to accept what was going on and get serious about the situation. At this point, I knew nothing good was going to happen if I didn't.

There was a paramedic on duty at work so I went to the First Aid station. The paramedic told me what I knew he would. The symptoms had advanced so he told me I had to go to the emergency room. I could feel my throat closing and my chest tightening which meant my airway was closing. This made it challenging to breathe and talk, of course. Obviously this was now becoming a real problem. Thanks to a kind and extremely caring co-worker, I was driven to the hospital. This was against the paramedic's advice and out of sheer stubbornness on my part. Even though I knew quite well how serious the situation was becoming, I was bent on down playing it for some reason. I've been admonished by doctors for doing this in the past. They have always told me to call 911 and be transported by ambulance.

We want to think we are in control and can manage situations, but it's important to recognize when something is not within our ability to control. This was one I should never have tried to manage. Ambulances exist for a reason. They are equipped with lights and sirens in order to pass through intersections, allowing you to bypass red lights in emergency situations. They are manned with trained personnel to assist and administer much needed medication prior to reaching the hospital. Just imagine being in your friend's car, getting stuck in traffic while your throat is closing, breathing through your nose only, and wondering if you will reach the hospital in time. We didn't get stuck in traffic, but we could have is the point. I'm grateful we got to the emergency room without incident. Even though it was a very short distance from my office to the hospital, I never should have put myself in further danger by going there in a car instead of an ambulance.

By the time we arrived at the ER, my chest had tightened up so much and my throat was virtually all the way closed, so I could barely speak. As soon as I whispered to the nurse I was having an allergic reaction, she ushered me straight to the back. That's the seriousness of an anaphylactic reaction. When you walk in an ER and can bearly tell them you are having an anaphylactic reaction you will get expedited straight to the back. No line, no waiting!

There was only one other reaction worse than this one. Many years ago, when visiting my brother while he was stationed in Germany, I came in contact with salmon. Note I said, "came in contact with". I did not say I ate it. I touched a piece of cloth that, unbeknownst to me, had been used to wipe up a spill from a plate of salmon. Simply touching the cloth and then touching my face caused my throat to close, my tongue and my lips to swell. It was quite an interesting experience to be in Germany, call for an ambulance, and spend the evening in a German hospital when I don't speak German! My brother had wonderful friends who stayed with us at the house and went with us to the hospital to assist in translating. It was a blessing to have them there.

Although the symptoms in Germany years ago were worse than what was now happening days before Thanksgiving, the experience I had as a result of the medicine this time took things to new, unpleasant heights. Why the Epinephrine affected me so harshly this time I can't explain. Once the medicine started flowing through the IV, I could feel it travel straight up my arm and into my head. It was as if cold water was going through my veins and I could feel it moving. When the medicine reached my head, it felt like there were two tiny people in there. One was slightly above and behind my right ear, the other slightly above and behind my left ear. Each of them seemed to have razor sharp ice picks they were using to stab me in the head, as if trying to find their way out. This was not one or two quick jabs. This went on continuously, non-stop, for a period of approximately 15 minutes. Never in my life had the medicine done that to me. I thought I was going to die and I mean that in the most literal sense. The intense pain seemed to last forever. I thought my head was going to explode! All I could do was hold my head with both hands as tightly as possible and pray to God it would stop! The nerve pain I experienced at the beginning of the year was excruciating but somehow I knew it was not life threatening. This, on the other hand, was a completely different story. I honestly did not know if I would survive.

Why was this happening? Yes, I know the reaction was caused by cross-contamination, but I was asking the question on a deeper level. Is this really how my year, or possibly even my life, was going to end? "Lord, why so much?" All I had were questions and no answers. The word says, *"In all thy getting, get understanding."* *(Proverbs 4:7)* This is precisely what I so desperately wanted.

In the midst of my screams and cries, I found myself asking again, "Why?" In asking, I was looking for understanding. It was never a way of saying this shouldn't happen to me. I'm no better than the next person. Life throws unpleasant situations at everyone. I'm certainly not exempt from that. I do believe for everything God allows, there is a reason and I was looking for some insight as to what the reason for this crazy, painful year was all about. What am I supposed to glean from all of this? I even wondered if this was a situation like with Job in the Bible. He was tested to see if he would still love God even if all his possessions and family were taken away from him, and his health put in jeopardy. Was I being tested in a similar manner? I realize Job lost everything and I knew I had not, but the principle matter is what I wondered about. The nurses had promised me the sharp, stabbing pain would go away after about fifteen minutes, and it did. God bless them! They were so compassionate and coached me through the entire process. Finally, after being there four to five hours, I was released. I was ready to get out of there and ready to be done with hospitals. 2013 had provided me with more opportunities to visit various hospitals than I would have ever imagined possible. If I never saw the inside of another hospital, I'd be a happy girl.

The next day, I was able to stay home and simply rest and recover. The word recover is being used quite loosely here. I surely had not rebounded from the experience after just one day. To think, feel, and believe you are about to leave this earth left me a bit dazed and numb.

Icing On The Cake

CHAPTER

11

Several years ago, Iyanla Vanzant published a book called **Value in the Valley.** In every low point in our lives, there is something of value to gain from the valley experiences we will have. For all of the bad, negative, physical and emotional pain 2013 brought my way, there was something good that came from every situation. There was a lesson, a blessing, a new perspective, or something else positive hidden within each. After the death of my co-worker a grief counselor came to our office. One thing she said which made a lasting impression for me was, "What did you learn from that person?" At the time, I didn't quite understand what she meant. He was an electrician. I have no skills in that area, nor had I ever asked him to teach me any. As time went by, I think I began to see what she meant. What I learned from him was to appreciate life. He lived life to the fullest and was happy while doing it. His work schedule was not ideal, nor the working conditions sometimes, but you wouldn't be able to tell that by the way he approached each work day.

When we lost Ms. Bernie, I realized how important it is to value the time you have with someone. Our visits could be short sometimes, but they were power-packed! We talked, laughed, prayed, ate, and often times started that cycle over again in the same visit. What I learned most from Ms. Bernie's life is God honors sacrifice but not selfishness. Though she never said that to me, her life exemplified it. She would sacrifice all she had; her time, her energy, her money, and her home, if someone needed it. God honored that and it was evident because she was so at peace with life. Her life was by no means easy, just like yours and mine are not, but she felt blessed. She walked blessed. She talked blessed. She was blessed. And if you knew her, you knew this to be true.

I have learned things no longer conquer me; I conquer things. This is what the Lord revealed to me and in me at the beginning of the journey in 2013. Starting with the time my eyes felt as if they were going to pop out of my head, I was able – through Him – to conquer the pain and render it nonexistent.

Everything that year came one right after the other. There was no time to recover from the last situation before the next one came. Through all that took place, I learned as long as I have Him in me, I have all the power I need to not only survive, but thrive as well! Thrive is exactly what I set out to do.

My surgery took place on February 21st and I was back to work on March 6th. I consider it yet another blessing to have been able to go back to work so soon. I had been home for nearly two months so it was physically challenging to work all day. The doctor put me on light duty and half days initially. It took a few weeks to build my stamina back up but I gave it my all. After the way the Lord had blessed me to come through the surgery, I was eager to get back on my feet. I felt I owed that to Him in return. It didn't matter that I no longer had clothes that fit properly because of the weight I lost in those two months. I was going to work! My first day back, I remember laughing because I had to pin my pants on both sides of my waist to make them fit. I still didn't care. I didn't hurt anymore, nor did I ache. I was simply weak from such a long period of inactivity. Going back to work as soon as I could was another way to praise God and acknowledge what He had done for little ol' me.

I could have stayed home a while longer. In fact, many wondered why I went back to work so early. Upon my return, some shared stories with me of their friends who had similar procedures done. The general consensus among them was I must have had a great doctor in order for me to be doing so well, so soon after the procedure. Each and every time I had the opportunity, I proudly let them know I did have a great doctor and his name was Jesus! There was no shame on my part and I know full well this is why He continues to bless me. The experiences of 2013 have taught me to be bold when it comes to acknowledging Him and the great things He has done in my life! He kept me, carried me, led me, and guided me through it all.

Another thing I was eager to do was get back to church. I had not been for two months and I missed it. The first Sunday I was able, I was there! One of the ladies took a picture of me after service and I liked the way it came out. She later emailed it to me and told me she took the liberty to Photoshop the scar from my neck. I didn't mind and appreciated it. I had become a bit self-conscious about it.

I liked the picture so well that I asked her to print a couple copies so that I could send one to each of my parents. The following Sunday at church, she handed me an envelope that contained the prints I requested. When I got home and opened the envelope I heard the Lord speak to me clear as day, "Don't erase your testimony." This time I hadn't even asked a question, but He had something to say in the matter for sure! Needless to say, I asked her to print copies of the original picture and those are the ones I sent to my parents not the edited version.

Be careful not to erase your testimony either. When God brings us through something, He does it in part for us. The testimony of it, however, is always intended to help someone else and to give Him the glory He is due. If He has blessed you by delivering you from something, you don't have to brag about it, but be sure you don't hide from it either. After all, it's not about us anyway. It's about His goodness, His mercy, and His grace. Overcoming our trials is what gives us a testimony. Sharing them will allow us to help others as they go through similar ones. We can help them understand what it will take to get through it because we've already come through. Erasing the scar from the picture would have been a measure of disrespect toward God and He surely did not deserve that. It wasn't because of me I was standing tall and strong in that picture, looking healthy and happy. It was because of Him!

The most significant thing I learned from the experiences of 2013 is people are the icing on the cake of my life. Yellow cake can be good all by itself, but when you slap a nice thick layer of chocolate icing on top, it is so much better! Red velvet cake is pretty delicious by itself but with cream cheese icing on it (and in the middle, too), it makes the cake much more enjoyable. It's the same with the people in my life who are close to me. I could squeak by without them, but I thank God for them because my life is so much better with them! There were many people in my corner all through my challenging year of 2013. God had me cradled in the palm of His hand every step of the way, so I would have survived without them being there. How wonderful it was, however, that I didn't have to! No matter how much faith a person has, everyone needs encouragement from time to time. I count it a blessing to have had such a supportive group of people around when I needed them most.

I could hear the concern in my dad's voice every time he called to check on me while I was sick and in pain. I knew it bothered him that he couldn't be with me when I was dealing with the nerve/disc issue. He knew that type of pain first-hand because he had dealt with it a few years earlier.

My mother called virtually every day to check on me. That is to be expected of a mother, nothing special about that I'm sure you'll agree. In those calls though, we got closer than we had been before. She was a source of strength and encouragement for me. We talked about things we had never spoken about. She reminded me there is power in the name of Jesus we can call on in our prayers. Friendships were strengthened. One friend in particular was a God-send. She and I had only been friends for a couple of years when all of this took place, but she was there as if we had been friends forever. I don't recall ever asking her to do anything for me. She always seemed to know when to offer. She volunteered to take me to the pre-op appointment before the surgery. She also picked me up from the hospital after the actual surgery. Valentine's Day was one week before the operation. I was so helpless prior to surgery. I wasn't able to drive and by this time, I felt like I had bothered my friends and family enough.

Yet, one day while talking with her on the phone, I mentioned that I felt bad that Valentine's Day was the next day and I didn't have anything to give my daughter or son. It didn't matter to me that he was almost 30. He was there at the house recuperating from his knee surgery and I wouldn't leave him out. You know a mother is always, first and foremost, thinking about her children. She told me she would be happy to go grab a few things and bring them to me. I did not want to send her out of her way, so I told her no. It was a school night and I was sure she had plenty to do that evening with her family. She said she didn't mind and I knew she meant it sincerely. She insisted it was not a problem, so I accepted her kind offer. She and her children went shopping for gifts and cards I could give to my family. They drove 30 miles to my house so I would have something to give the next day. I was extremely thankful she so willingly went out of her way to help me.

Ms. Bernie was there for me as my spiritual sounding board. One day, during the ordeal of my health, I felt a heavy spirit of condemnation come over me. I was about to turn forty-six and had no husband. Divorce was not something I ever thought I would experience, let alone twice by this time. I recounted every mistake

I felt I had made the past twenty years of my life and didn't feel too good about myself. How could my first marriage, which lasted ten years and resulted in a child, have fallen apart and ended in divorce?

We were both good people. We both loved our daughter. Wasn't that enough to have gotten us over the rough times? Were ten years that easy to throw away? Was it mostly my fault? Or, was it simply just not meant to be? Was the second, short-lived marriage a mistake from the beginning? Is that why it didn't work? Or, had we exerted our own wills and rushed into the marriage before the Lord blessed it to be so?

I'm thankful I was able to recall **Romans 8:1** which reminds us **"There is therefore now no condemnation to them which are in Christ Jesus, who walk not after the flesh, but after the Spirit."** Since I knew what I was feeling was not of God, I didn't want to hold on to it. But I would need some help, so I called Ms. Bernie knowing she would show compassion, pray with me, and get me back in a good head space. That was what I really needed – to get back into a good place. The things I found myself thinking about were not new. I had pondered those a time or two the past few years. The intense sadness over them, however, was new. I could only attribute this to the pillbox of meds I was taking to stay somewhat comfortable. Side effects from medicines are real and should be monitored closely, especially when taking them for an extended period of time.

When I initially called, she wasn't available, so I left a message on her voicemail. How she understood anything I was saying is still a mystery to me! I cried the entire time while leaving the message. After she heard the message, she called back immediately. As I knew she would, she made me feel better. Simply hearing her voice helped to calm me and give me a little peace. She was blessed like that. She could say, "Oh baby, what's the matter?" and just the sweet nature of her tone, I'd start feeling a change on the inside, like things might actually be okay.

Even the young man who took me from work to the hospital that November was a huge blessing and I consider him part of the icing on the cake of my life. I was going to drive myself to the hospital that day but he wouldn't let me, and I'm glad he didn't. His caring, compassionate nature helped me to relax and remain calm. Some would say, because he was a new employee at the time, he was doing an act of kindness as a means to prove himself or 'get in good' with a senior staff member. That was not the case at all. He was being his genuine self.

During times of crisis, but in life overall, surrounding yourself with people who have your best interest at heart keeps you encouraged. They are blessings from above; appreciate them and see them for the icing on the cake of your life they have been sent to be. God has orchestrated their place in your life..

I'm grateful for all the good people, friends and family, who stepped in during my time of extreme need. My independence was lost. There wasn't much I was able to do for myself or my family.

I only had use of my right arm and hand. Not being able to cook, clean, wash dishes effectively (I don't do the dishwasher), or drive was something I had not experienced before. Frankly, cooking and driving probably weren't wise things to try and do anyway because of the amount and strength of pain medicines I was on. Being dependent was not something I was comfortable with but I was in a state of need. So many people called, sent flowers, cards, and food via delivery services, or dropped food off personally. Yet, if it had not been for my niece, I don't know how I would have managed.

I could never diminish what the others did, for their support was deeply and sincerely appreciated. This young lady, however, would grocery shop, cook, wash dishes, and do light cleaning. I don't even recall doing my own laundry so she probably did that, too. When my daughter contacted her in the middle of the night saying I was in pain, she came right over and took me to the emergency room. She took my prescriptions and got them filled. She was also the one who took me to the hospital the morning of the surgery. She didn't complain. She never told me no or she was too busy, or it was too early in the morning for her. She epitomizes the family first mentality and I love that about her. Grateful seems to be an insufficient, weak word when

I think about how much of a help she was. Just knowing I could call on her at any time was reassuring.

For all of the shadows of darkness that seemed to linger around me in the valley season of 2013, I am thankful the Lord blessed me to be able to see all of the good. Without all of the wonderful people who came to my aid, loved me through the turmoil, supported and encouraged me until things got better, the cake of my life would be pretty plain. They made each day during that time sweeter which helped me endure. I thank God that each of them allowed themselves to be used by Him. They all had choices and could have chosen to watch from the sidelines and hope I survived. Instead, they got in the game of life with me to ensure I survived, and for that I am grateful.

CHAPTER

12 | Settled

This most recent stint in the emergency room did not prevent me from going home for Thanksgiving. What a bright spot in my year that vacation was! It was so cold there but I loved it! One day it was only nineteen degrees with a wind chill of minus one hundred! Okay, so the wind chill part is an exaggeration but it was nineteen degrees and I felt it. It was beautiful! The cold air made my skin feel refreshed. While others at home were running from the cold, I relished in it, looking for any excuse to be outside. When friends and family visit me in Florida, they reference being outside 'soaking up the sunshine'. Well, I was up North soaking up all the cold, frigid air.

As I thought it would be, the trip home was exactly what I needed. The time with my family helped me to heal a little from all that I had been dealing with throughout the year. New and fond memories were created that will stay with me a lifetime, in particular, with my mother. My Mom has always had very definite likes and dislikes, and typically doesn't deviate from them. I told her that I had been making pumpkin bread and wanted her to try it. She said that she would so I made one for her and she loved it! It may sound like an inconsequential thing but my mother passed away fifteen months later. That was the last holiday I spent with her. It is indeed a special memory for me now.

Part of my ten-day visit was spent in Chesapeake, VA with my goddaughter. There were many things about my vacation that I was looking forward to and spending time with her ranked high on the list. When she was little, we spent a great deal of quality time with one another. Once I moved to Florida, our visits were far too infrequent compared to what we were used to. Now she was a young woman, living on her own. This would be my first opportunity to see her apartment. The visit was supposed to be a surprise but she figured out I was coming. She just didn't know exactly when. We made the most of our time together before it was cut short.

The weather was expected to turn for the worse. After visiting with her, I was scheduled to drive to West Virginia where I would spend Thanksgiving with my Mom, Dad, and brother. In order to get ahead of the storm, I needed to leave almost a full day early. As soon as I left her apartment, the adventure began. I got stuck in traffic. No big deal, it happens. I was almost in a car accident after the traffic cleared up. No big deal, the Lord protected me. It began to sleet. No big deal, I'll just slow down. It began to hail. Okay, a little bit of a big deal now, but I'll manage. When I made it to the mountains of West Virginia, fog set in and I could only see five feet in front of me, if that. This was the first time I could recall ever being truly afraid to drive. I felt stress, anxiety, and worry rising up in me. I prayed like nobody's business in that vehicle. A thought even crossed my mind to pull over and have my dad and brother come get me. After thinking about it more, I decided not to. I did not want to put them in danger on the roads. So, the Lord and I had a good, long talk. I was reminded of all He had helped me through since January. He assured me that He would not leave me now.

I pressed on and maneuvered through the fog, dodged the deer, and made it safely to our small town. My brother greeted me outside in the blinding weather to help guide me as I backed my rental SUV down the driveway. I was so relieved to finally be there. The trip was torturous and had taken much longer because of the dangerous conditions. All I could think was, 'Thank you Lord, I made it!' About that time, while my brother guided me down the driveway with hand signals, I backed right into his SUV! Well...I made it, but not necessarily without incident! No major damage was done to either vehicle but it did provide us with many laughs the next few days.

Even though I couldn't articulate it at the time, that trip home for Thanksgiving needed to be a respite. I just needed to be in good company where I felt safe, secure, and cared for. I wanted to laugh because I had cried so much that year. I needed to go with the flow; I didn't want to make any decisions. I needed to be on auto pilot. I didn't want to have to think too hard because I had spent the past several months thinking; trying to come up with an explanation for all that was going on constantly in my world.

When my family would ask my preference on anything, even something as simple as input on the side dishes for Thanksgiving dinner, it didn't matter to me. The standard response became, "it doesn't matter; whatever you want". This in and of itself should have been an indicator that something wasn't quite right with me because I always have an opinion and certainly have preferences, especially in regards to food. If I was asked the same question twice I could feel myself getting annoyed. I did not want to make any decisions.

Again, this was not at all typical of me. I'm certain that my family did not understand why I was responding to things in this way. It's not that I didn't want to explain. The fact of the matter was I hadn't gotten to the point where even I fully understood what was going on with me. I knew that I was worn out in every possible way but I didn't realize yet how that affected so many aspects of my personality, interactions with people, and my responses to life.

If you were to judge by appearances only, you would not have been able to tell what turmoil I was in on the inside. On the outside, I looked fine. As a matter of fact, I look back at pictures of myself from this Thanksgiving getaway and I am amazed. God kept me! For as much as I may have felt like I was falling apart, He was keeping me together. That may be another reason why no one understood how deeply the events of that year had affected me...they couldn't see evidence of it. It is by the grace of God only that I did not look like what I was going through!

When it was all said and done the getaway rejuvenated me and after ten days of carefree living, it was time to go back to Florida. Not only did the cold air refresh my skin, the time away from my life and the time with my family refreshed my spirit. I felt good again. I felt happy again. All of the craziness that was my life for the first eleven months of 2013 was over.

Although I was quite ready for a new beginning and ready for the challenges of the year to be behind me, there was one more challenge to come. Even now, many years after the fact, I still have a hard time believing so much took place in the span of twelve months, better known as 2013. In December 2013, I came down with the stomach flu. Not every case is severe enough to warrant time in the emergency room but this one certainly did.

I woke up one morning and knew something wasn't quite right. My stomach felt nauseous. I racked my brain trying to recall what I may have eaten the night before that would have my stomach upset. It was all pretty basic stuff. I was bound and determined to work through it, yet getting dressed was turning out to be a difficult task. I didn't have any energy. It didn't matter. I was claiming that I would not get sick even though I knew I probably had a temperature as well. Not now, and certainly not again! It was the week before Christmas for goodness sake. It took me three times longer than normal to get ready for work but I forged on.

During the drive to work, I prayed what I was feeling was not the flu. If it was, I wasn't going to claim it. 'It will pass', I thought to myself. I wanted to believe it was just an upset stomach from something I had eaten. My prayer was that it would work its way out of my system soon. When I arrived at work, I couldn't even park in the garage as we are supposed to. The garage was only a block from my office but I knew I couldn't walk that far because I was feeling very weak. Instead, I parked right in front of the building and still had to sit in the car for several minutes. The mere thought of walking from the car inside the building exhausted me. It took every bit of strength I could muster up to make the journey inside.

By the time I made it to my office at 10am I knew I had made a terrible mistake by coming in. There was nothing I could do but ask the Lord to give me enough strength to make it back to my car to go home. What had I been thinking? I was in denial...again. I knew that's what it was but I didn't want to accept it. I didn't want to be sick again. It took an hour before I gained enough strength to leave.

The mere thought of eating or drinking actually made my stomach feel queasier, so I hadn't had anything all morning. Typically, by 11am, I would have already consumed my first cup of coffee and be in the process of making lunch plans. None of that seemed like a good idea but I was getting thirsty so I drank some water. As it turned out, it wasn't a good idea. Water would not stay down. If I drank even a sip of water, get a bag ready because it was going to be coming back up in exactly fifteen minutes! It was like clockwork and this went on for several hours. As I consider myself a lady, I won't go into any further details of that nasty experience. Just know that it was not nice, cute, or polite and let your imagination do the rest.

As the day went on, I became dehydrated from not being able to keep anything in me. I had no choice but to go to the hospital. Thankfully, my daughter was home and could drive me there. Although she doesn't say much, the concern she felt was all over her face. I felt bad for getting sick in the car while she drove, but of course I couldn't help it.

When we arrived at the hospital, she thought it would be a good idea to drop me off at the entrance to the emergency room but I wouldn't let her. She didn't want me to walk far, but that would mean she would have to go park the car by herself. At that time, she only had her permit, not her actual license. A licensed driver was supposed to be in the car with her anytime she drove. I told her, "I'll be fine, park in the garage." Once parked, I looked at the distance I'd have to walk to the emergency room entrance and realized it was impossible. There simply was no way I could walk that far. She was right and I should have listened to her in that instance. She drove back to the entrance, dropped me off, parked the car by herself, and then met me inside afterwards.

This was now my sixth hospital visit of the year. 2013 just would not leave me alone for some reason. I was sick, but I was also numb. I was numb to the entire process. Registering at the ER intake desk; needles; IVs; cold hospital cubicles; copays, I was numb to all of it. Actually, there was no hospital copay required this time. I learned that after visit number five. I paid the copay they asked for on my fifth trip when I had the allergic reaction, but it was later returned to me. Apparently, I had reached my out of pocket maximum but was unaware of it at the time.

While in the emergency room, hooked up to a bag of fluids, I couldn't help wondering what all of this was about. Six trips to the hospital, the loss of people I cared about, the painful blow I received from the young man I loved as my son – why did all of this happen in the twelve short months of 2013. Never before had I experienced a year like this. Then I remembered something I had heard long ago: The enemy fights you the hardest when you are closest to God's plan for your life. I really had to think on that for a while. Could that be what was going on? Was the enemy fighting me so viciously this year because God had a marvelous plan for my life and I was getting close to recognizing it? Were these attacks designed to distract me from what God had coming my way? As my grandparents may have said, "I reckoned that might be the case." From that moment on, I didn't feel weary anymore. My body still felt weak from the illness I was fighting, but my spirit was being lifted. I actually found myself laughing. I thought I had finally figured out what all of the pain and suffering had been for. It was the enemy's plan to lessen my faith, to make me question God and His love for me. The funny thing was that it didn't work, and that's why I laughed! My faith had not wavered. I never once questioned if God was with me or if He loved me. Yes, I did ask Him a time or two what the purpose was behind it all, but I never felt like He left me or didn't love me. I laughed because I was winning. The enemy was taking his absolute best shot at me and not one thing he tried was working! When I felt like I had this all figured out that day in the ER, it was another opportunity to praise the

Lord! He had sustained me through it all and it only deepened my relationship with Him. Yes, I was tired and I was tired of being tired, but I was still feeling quite victorious!

In the early stages of developing this book, it was suggested to me that I not include the story of my sixth trip to the hospital. I was told that the readers would be tired of hearing my ER stories. That was exactly the point I needed to make! If you, as the reader, are tired of reading it, wouldn't you realize how tired I was of living it? Wouldn't you realize at that point how much faith it took for me to survive it all, to not give up, and to not quit? These are not just words on paper; this was my life for the twelve months known as 2013. I was tired. I was emotionally beat up. At points along the way, I was discouraged. I fought back feelings of depression but I had to stand tall and strong even when I wasn't sure I could. There were times when I was completely depleted physically and emotionally, yet, because of my faith, I knew I would eventually be okay.

We really have to be careful who we allow to help us with certain things, especially if it's a Kingdom assignment. Writing this book is my assignment from the Lord and I couldn't allow their feedback to hinder what I knew I was supposed to write. Did their opinion cause me to momentarily question the content? It sure did, but guess what? I knew better than to let the feeling of doubt take root. I knew they meant well but they were not plugged in spiritually to the assignment I had been given. All along, I've taken my direction from my Heavenly Father and I decided to continue with that and disregard the suggestion.

Just as the Lord gave me guidance on what to include, He gave me guidance on what not to include. There were several other experiences in 2013 that magnified the intensity of all that occurred. I am a single mother of a beautiful, smart, creative, talented, funny, and strong willed teenage daughter. That alone comes with a litany of challenges. Helping her navigate through her high school years; watching her beautiful, delicate heart get broken over her first love; peer pressure; interest from and in boys; and her desire for independence certainly would have been enough to keep me occupied during 2013.

The one person I believed to be my best friend for life, based on our twenty-year friendship, exited my life in the middle of the chaos of 2013 and I have no idea why. We had supported and encouraged each other through so much over the years. Realizing that someone I thought I could count on forever wasn't going to be there was hard. I had looked up to her; modeled my single parenting after hers as best I could. When the dynamics of a twenty-year relationship change, seemingly overnight, it can leave you hurt and bewildered.

But even in that, the Lord showed me a great lesson. We are not to model ourselves after anyone other than Jesus and it is only in Him that we should put our trust.

Additionally, I glossed over the finite details of what happened with my son prior to asking him to leave my home because some things need to be told, and some don't. So yes, I included the story of the last trip to the hospital because I was supposed to. The Lord let me know that someone needed to read it because it will help them stand strong in the midst of their trials when they think they can't take anything else. I was feeling very beat down at that point but He was well able to sustain me the same way He will sustain you!

In some respects I feel as if I lost a year of my life in 2013. I was in pure survival mode and not really living. We've all had to do that before – operate in survival mode to make it through a storm in life – but I never envisioned I would have to do it for twelve straight months! Maybe you've had to endure for an even longer period of time than I, and, your suffering even greater. The length of time nor the degree is not the main factor. Our deep-rooted faith and the love God has for us is the key factor. He brought me through and He will do the same for you.

No one knows how deeply the events of that year affected me. How could they? I've not been able to find words true enough to explain it. I was tired and worn out as well as emotionally depleted. The physical, emotional, and psychological warfare accompanied by all of the grief, loss, and rejection left me empty. It was too much to understand as I was living it, so surely there was no way I could explain it to anyone other than the Lord. It was up to us, just He and I, to work it out, and that's just what we did. Through prayers, tears, questions, and answers we did exactly that!

After leaving the hospital the last time in 2013, I remember telling close friends and family members that the incidents of the year had been designed by the enemy to keep me from what God would be bringing my way soon. I was so confident and comfortable with that, and was able to end the year with a sense of peace. None of the weapons formed against me had prospered!

There was even a feeling of excitement when I pondered the great things that would be in store for me. The life I lived, or shall I say endured, in 2013 still doesn't seem real. It doesn't seem possible.

It doesn't seem feasible that one person can withstand so much in a relatively short period of time and still be sane. But it is possible. It is feasible. I am still sane and to God be the glory!!! Even though I thought I had finally gotten the answer to my question of why it all happened, I sensed that it wasn't supposed to end there. At the beginning of the next New Year, January 2014, there was a pulling in my spirit to write it all down. For Heaven's sake, who wants to relive a year like that by recounting it in written detail?

Above and beyond that, what was writing it going to do? The questions were starting to pour in again and, just like before, I didn't have the answers.

One thing I did know was that I needed to stay obedient to what was in my spirit. Some call it intuition while others refer to it as a gut feeling. I know it was the leading of the Holy Spirit, but I wasn't sure of the reason. I presumed it was going to be a therapy project for me. When I was young, I used writing as self-prescribed therapy. Often times, if I felt I could not verbally express myself, I would write letters instead. Sometimes I wrote just to get things out but never let a soul read what had been written. It worked well for me. I concluded this was likely the reason I was being guided to write my story. I had wounds from many of the things that occurred in 2013. Maybe writing would bring the complete healing I needed. With no outline and no bullet pointed notes, I opened my laptop one night in bed and began to type. Eight full pages of text had been typed before I knew it, yet that didn't come close to making a dent in covering the events of the year. By this time, I had become intrigued. As I sat and thought about the sum total of the year, I began to realize, I had quite a bit to say about 2013. When I began to see how the Lord moved in my life from the beginning of the year until the very end, I haphazardly began asking myself if this writing assignment might benefit others. As quickly as I entertained the idea, I somewhat dismissed it. I have to say 'somewhat' because all the while, the Holy Spirit kept nudging me, and I began to feel that it was for the purpose of sharing my story with others. If there was any way possible that it could serve as encouragement for someone else, I considered it a blessing. If my testimony of faith and obedience could inspire someone, anyone, I was willing to share it.

My first thought was to continue getting it all out on paper. My second thought was to keep this to myself. I didn't want to tell anyone that I 'thought' I was writing a book, just in case it really did end up being a therapy project, intended just for me. I wanted the luxury of getting it out of my head and onto paper without pressure from people asking, "When will it be done?" I wanted to move at God's direction and not man's.

Incredible things will happen when we allow ourselves to be spiritually obedient. It never ceases to amaze me when the Lord speaks to me so clearly and in the most interesting ways. In the process of 'getting it out of my head and on paper,' I received the real answer to my year-long question. It was so powerful, yet incredibly simple, and spoken in basic terms. While typing out more of my story one night, the Lord took control of my hands. One word at a time, He showed me why it was necessary for me to have experienced so much during that period of my life. When the words were on the screen in front of me it was such a moving, life changing moment.

" I did it "
to settle you.

Now, I was beyond amazed and intrigued. Did this really just happen? Did He just take control of my hands and use them to type words on the screen that were not even in my train of thought? I lost my breath and my heart stopped beating for a couple of seconds. What was happening was too surreal for words! I sat there completely stunned for a few moments. I can't say that I regained my composure after those few moments, because I didn't. My emotions shifted from being stunned to being overwhelmed with gratitude. And for me, at times like this, my gratitude comes out in pure tears.

I sat there that night on my bed, with my laptop open and the tears fell on the keyboard. There was so much significance in all of this.

1. The Lord proved to be with me yet again.

2. He loved me enough to answer the question I had been asking throughout the year.

3. For Him to do it in that manner was incredibly humbling. He literally used my hands to deliver His message to me.

4. There was so much meaning for me in those few words on the computer screen.

5. The answer He gave was designed to help me grow in my walk with Him, which, above all else confirmed for me without a shadow of a doubt that I belong to Him!

6. It was a pure and true revelation from above.

"I did it to settle you." Those six words likely won't mean much, if anything, to you because they are the answer to my question. Your question and circumstances are probably different than mine, so your answer from Him will be different. For me, however, it was what I had longed to hear for many, many months.

And, after the shock of the experience wore off and I re-read the words on the screen in front of me, I began to ponder the meaning. One thing came to mind instantly, but I am continually gaining insight into what He meant. I had to ask Him to help show me exactly what He meant by "I did it to settle you". I wanted to be sure I understand it in full detail.

My initial thought was that He had to settle me in my emotions. Without hesitation, I have to admit that I have lived life operating in and out of emotions. My feelings were always worn on my shoulder for all to see. I let things offend me, sometimes only to realize later that no offense was intended. When I did not agree with something, I felt it was my right to speak up accordingly. When something happened that made me sad, I believe I carried the sadness longer than necessary because I didn't know how to process the feelings and put them in proper perspective. There were reactions to things, responses, and decisions that I frequently made while in the heat of the moment. I could be very easily knocked off course by anger, frustration, and resentment, lack of patience, and virtually any other negative emotion or feeling. It wasn't just negative emotions that I would act off of though. I can identify specific mistakes I made from being caught up in the temporary hype of a situation and let it persuade me into believing it was right for me when it wasn't.

If it sounded good, sign me up. I hadn't learned the importance of putting things before God in prayer to see if it was something I was supposed to be involved with.

Before the events of 2013 took place, I needed to be in control. If I could not control the outcome, I feared it. But, through the events of that year, the Lord showed me that I am not and cannot be in control all the time. That's His job and I believe He wanted me to learn that through those experiences.

Being a leader is more my personality than a follower. During 2013, He provided me with multiple opportunities to follow His leading because, if left to my own decision-making, things would not have worked out in my favor. At times I didn't understand, but I followed anyway.

You probably could have classified part of my personality as being a fighter. Not so much in the physical sense, but in terms of standing firm and strong for what I believed was true, right, fair, and just. I didn't shy away from opportunities to voice my opinion, in an effort to set straight the record of a wrong-doing. But there comes a time when it is in our best interest to let the Lord fight our battles. My fight now needs to be reserved for Kingdom purposes in order to fulfill my destiny.

I don't have such a strong need to defend myself anymore. I did that a lot out of insecurity. I had to prove to people who I was, when in reality, I wasn't quite sure myself for many years. I can see now that it's no longer necessary for me to do that. I am very secure in who I am because the Lord has shown me. Through the battles of 2013, He was with me the entire time and manifested Himself in my life in undeniable ways. He wouldn't do that if I didn't belong to Him. So, as a child of the Most High God, it no longer matters what people say or think! I now leave it up to the individual to figure out who I am to them, because I know who I am to God!

I wanted to fix things but that was not my job in many cases. God is the author and finisher. Who am I to determine how things need to be fixed or finished?

He had to settle me to help me understand that it is only by Him I am able to do and be anything if I am to help build the Kingdom. The only way He could use me to the fullest was less of me and more of Him in control of my life. So, He settled me.

In His infinite wisdom, He chose to line up the situations of 2013 for them to occur in rapid succession to let me know it was time for me to grow beyond my emotions. It was because of His love for me that He chose to do that. If He didn't love me, He would have continued to allow me to squander my life away by living through feelings and not Him. Things happen; life happens. The beautiful thing is that He has given us all that we need to handle everything that comes our way, but it's up to us to draw on it when the time comes. He had to do something to settle me, since I wasn't grasping hold to the concept I just shared with you.

It is important to understand, I am by no means suggesting that Ms. Bernie or my co-worker's time here on earth ended just so that I could grow and mature. The reality of life is that Ms. Bernie was going to pass at some point, and so was he. Health issues happen to everyone, I'm not exempt from that. We've all had family members hurt us and friends desert us. What the Lord was able to do was use all of these things that were going to happen anyway, line them up in His perfect order to serve a purpose. If they were going to happen anyway, why not let something good come from them? None of them felt good as they occurred, but collectively they worked together to serve some good. Here is where we have to remember *Romans 8:28 which says "All things work together for the good of those who love the Lord and are called according to His purpose."* Many of us have read it and we can quote it with proficiency, but do we have any real idea of what it means in our lives? Can you see that working out in your life right now? One thing has to happen so that the next thing can happen, and so on, in order to get to a specific end result where God can be glorified and we can grow in Him!

He had made His point and I received it gladly. There was significance for me within those six words. Funny, isn't it? They aren't even complex words..."I did it to settle you". Individually, they are as basic as can be. Yet, combined together, they held the key to my future and how I would be able to proceed through the rest of my life. I had been seeking an answer to my question and thought it would be mind-boggling; too deep to understand. It wasn't.

To say that He has reached perfection in my life with the settling process would be a falsehood. I am a work in progress, as we all are. We won't ever reach perfection here but we can pursue it every day. Obviously, I do still have emotions. Actually, I feel things very deeply. I've been known to cry at the drop of a hat if I see or hear something that touches me. Being settled doesn't mean that I am emotionless or that I am incapable of being upset. What it means is that I do not have to act out of my emotions anymore. Instead of living my life unbalanced, being moved by the feeling of the moment, the Lord has shown me that it is in my best interest to live a balanced, steadfast life grounded in the faith which sustained me through much turmoil. I've not become some perfect person just by gaining this insight, but I am yielding to what He has taught me. Therefore, I try to be much more cognizant of how I handle things. Everything does not have to move me off course. I will still make mistakes because I'm human. But I'm a better and happier human for making the effort to live according to His guidance.

He is still revealing to me the full extent of what He meant by being settled. As time goes by, I catch glimpses of what the Lord is showing me that needs to be adjusted or purged from my life in order to be who He wants me to be. I'm learning, in order to not only survive but to thrive by faith, there are some things that must be taken to the altar and left there. For each of us, those things may be different. For me, I had to leave fear, insecurity, and doubt at the altar. I feared the unknown and anything that I could not control. I was insecure in who I was as a child of God so I couldn't walk in the authority that has been provided so graciously to all of us. Although, I have always been quite decisive and confident in taking the lead with decision-making, I would secretly second-guess myself afterwards. At times, I doubted if I was capable of doing what I felt I was being called to do.

When you leave something at the altar that means you've given it to God to help you. It does not mean that you won't have moments when you're tempted to take them back. It will take a conscientious effort every day to fight that temptation. Leave it with Him. He is more than capable and willing to work it out on your behalf.

It has been amazing to see how being settled has shown itself in so many areas of my life. For example, there is one very charismatic television preacher that I have always liked to watch. His messages used to move me because they struck a chord with me, emotionally.

I would get so hyped up while listening and watching the services on television. It was as if I needed to be moved emotionally instead of intellectually in order to grasp the message. That is no longer the case. Don't get me wrong, I still enjoy watching him, probably more now than before. He is dynamic and anointed without a shadow of a doubt. The difference now is that preaching does not have to appeal to me from an emotional standpoint in order for me to receive the message. Now I'm able to push beyond the hype and the messages seem to be absorbed better and stick with me longer. Emotions are feelings and feelings are fleeting. Being settled and having a foundation of faith is what sustains us, not feelings.

In the early stages of writing this book, I remember thinking that it was going to end up as a form of therapy for me. It turns out that it was. Had I not done as the Holy Spirit was leading me to do (write), I would not have received the answer that I needed. Had I not heard the answer directly from the Lord (that He did it to settle me), I would not have healed completely from all that I had endured. Having that revelation helped me to understand that it was all for a purpose, that I was unable to see, during that time. Knowing that it was not all in vain was critical in me being able to move forward in a positive way. Although none of those events were pleasant, I am not mad and I am not bitter. I am grateful that He loved me enough to settle me!

Had I known all of what was really going on as the events of 2013 were unfolding, I might have tried to intervene for one reason or another.

Would I have tried to help the Lord along the way to speed up the process? I probably would have. This is precisely why He doesn't always share His full plan with us, up front. He does not need our assistance! *"For as the heavens are higher than the earth, so are my ways higher than your ways, and my thoughts than your thoughts."* *(Isaiah 55:9)* He knew what He was doing. He didn't need any help from me!

When the challenges of life come now, I feel much stronger and better equipped to handle them. I don't feel invincible by any stretch of the imagination, but I have realized where my help comes from. *"I will lift up my eyes unto the hills, from whence cometh my help. My help cometh from the Lord, which made heaven and earth."* *(Psalm 121:1-2)* He had to show me this through a series of not so pleasant events in my life. In 2013, I felt like I was being beaten into submission and in essence, I was. God wanted me to submit to Him fully and not to my emotions or my feelings. The only way to do that was to put me in a place where I would have to rely on Him and Him alone.

It seemed as if my fight had been taken away, my strength was feigning, and eventually depleted altogether. It was all true and it was necessary for Him to do this. I apparently thought it was of my own strength that I was able to handle life. Maybe there was an incident along the way in my life where I got a little too full of myself that prompted Him to remind me that it is only because of Him in me that I was able to do anything at all. *"I can do all things through Christ which strengthens me." (Philippians 4:13)* I guess I got it twisted somewhere along the way, but thank God for loving me enough to put me back on track!

Even in my finances, things happened in 2013. Now, having been enlightened and settled, I understand that I don't have to get anxious about them. I don't welcome financial challenges but I no longer allow them to become bigger than my God's ability to help me through them. As a matter of fact, I heard the Lord tell me one day that "there is no credit in Heaven". I'm not making these things up. He speaks to me often like this. It would take Him and only Him to give me a message like that because I would never think of it myself. It is so contrary to how I was raised and taught to think. I was raised to be responsible with my finances and protect my credit rating. Well, guess what? Stuff happens and it's not the end of the world! It's really important that I convey, I have not thrown my fiscal responsibility out of the window by any means. All I'm saying is that I know things will happen even with our finances, but we don't have to react to the situation as if it is catastrophic. Besides that, I think the Lord was trying to remind me that His grace and favor has the ability to do more for me than the highest of credit scores!

"There is no credit in Heaven." Not only did that statement give me a little comfort in the situation I was working through, it gave me a glimpse at something else He may have been trying to remind me of: *Colossians 3:1-2 says "If ye then be risen with Christ, seek those things which are above, where Christ sitteth on the right hand of God. Set your affection on things above, not on things on the earth."* Unfortunately, that is precisely what I had been doing! The concern for my credit score was actually a form of affection and I was nurturing it in a sense. With His softly spoken words "there is no credit in Heaven", He reminded me of what was really important- - eternal things like HEAVEN, and not a worldly thing like credit!

I am glad that year of my life is over but at the same time, I am thankful that it happened. I had to experience it all, and in the precise order it was orchestrated to even have a chance of coming into the fullness of who Christ created me to be. If you're in the midst of your own personal storm and you're not quite sure what to do, I'd like to offer you an opportunity to go on your own faith journey. There is a 21-day faith journey journal that follows. If you are seeking answers, growth, or a deeper understanding of things that are occurring or have happened, I encourage you to take this journey. I am confident that He will show you things that only He can.

He answers our questions because that's the kind of God He is. He is a provider. Often times we think of Him being a provider only in terms of tangible things. He provides ALL that we need, including answers to questions. The key is to be patient and stay in the right place (spiritually) long enough to hear from Him when He's ready. Being willing to follow His gentle nudging is a key element, as well. What if I had never put my experiences on paper? I would still be presuming I had received the full and complete answer that evening in the emergency room when I had the flu. Now, in all honesty, I do believe that there are wonderful things in store for my life. The events of 2013, however, were orchestrated by God and not the enemy. They were meant for my good and not my harm. I believe that God had to settle me in order to prepare me for what is to come!

Through our obedience, He shows us what to do and what not to do; when to do it and when not to do it. He has spoken to me many, many times in the past and still does. There were times when I didn't recognize His voice for what it was. Sometimes, I mistake my wants and desires for His voice. I try diligently not to make that mistake anymore. I am learning how to stay in tune with Him. There are still areas of my life that I am trying to turn completely over to the Lord. At least, I understand now that I need to; that's step one! A work in progress is what I am and I believe I am on the right track. We don't become instantaneously perfected after a revelation. We won't ever be perfect. Our eyes are simply opened so that we can make a conscientious effort to adjust in the area(s) shown to us. Daily, I have to practice letting go in ALL areas of my life and allow God to lead me. It's not enough to submit in some ways; we have to be all in. Either we're going to trust and believe or we're not. The Bible even cautions us about straddling the fence: *Revelations 3:15-16 "I know thy works, that thou art neither cold nor hot: I would thou wert cold or hot. So then because thou art lukewarm, and neither cold nor hot, I will spue thee out of my mouth."*

It's not that I don't trust the Lord because He has surely shown me over and over again that it's only Him I can trust. Even if I didn't have a bounty of personal experiences to prove this, the word tells us the same in *Psalms 118:8 "It is better to trust in the Lord than put confidence in man."* The simple fact of the matter is we are weak vessels made strong only through Him. With practice and determination, I'll get there...and so will you!

You may never have a prophetic word spoken over your life by a Bishop, Pastor, Reverend, Deacon, or Elder and that's okay. God does not necessarily need to use them to deliver an in-season word to you. He can speak it directly into your spirit Himself. But maybe you have had an anointed man or woman of God prophesy things over your life. That's fine, too. People with the genuine gift of prophesy are indeed messengers for God. Receive the word He has for you because it will add meaning to your life. Whichever way His messages come, the key is to be alert and aware, ready to hear from

Him when He is ready to speak, and then being willing to act on it accordingly.

Someone once prophesied that, although I am small in stature, God would use me mightily in the Kingdom to help His people breakdown strongholds in their lives. Prayerfully, my openness with you, the information and real life experiences shared in these pages, combined with the journal that follows will serve as a spring board to begin that process for you. Let's claim that together in the name of JESUS!

Final Thought:

There are many people who have endured much more than I. I have come to realize that it is not what you go through, but how you go through it and what you get out of it that matters. That is the message I hope was conveyed in **Survival by Faith**.

21-Day Faith Journey Journal

My faith is what kept me through the most trying times of my life. While I was going through each trial and test I didn't completely understand that, however. I was simply in survival mode. What nourished my faith and allowed me to press on were the promises of God found in His powerful word, the Bible. ***"So then faith comes by hearing, and hearing by the word of God." (Romans 10:17)*** There were times when I relied on others to help encourage me and keep me uplifted, but there were plenty more times when I was by myself and had to encourage myself. The only successful way to do that was through the word.

While reading, one thing I began to realize is, in God, things are very definitive. "Shall" and "will" are used in the passages of His promises quite often. I was hard pressed to find references in the Bible where God said He 'might' do something. That was encouraging to me and I hope it will be for you as well, as you take this 21-day faith journey. With all of my heart, I believe this exercise will help you live the life that has been ordained for you!

Life is full of ups and downs, set-backs, wrong turns, and U-turns along the way, but you can control how they affect you. Your faith can be your passenger or the driver; the choice is yours to make! After reading the scripture for each day, pray about it, meditate on it, and make notes on what the Lord reveals to you and for you regarding it.

Embark on this 21-day journey with a spirit of expectancy and watch things begin to happen!

Blessings to you always!

Psalms 27:14

Day 1

Wait on the Lord: be of good courage and He shall strengthen thine heart: wait, I say, on the Lord.

_____

_____

_____

_____

_____

_____

_____

_____

_____

_____

_____

_____

_____

Isaiah 26:3

Day 2

Thou wilt keep him in perfect peace, whose mind is stayed on thee: because he trusteth in thee.

_____

_____

_____

_____

_____

_____

_____

_____

_____

_____

_____

_____

IICorinthians 12:9

Day 3

And He said unto me, My grace is sufficient for thee, for my strength is made perfect in weakness.

_____
_____
_____
_____
_____
_____
_____
_____
_____
_____
_____
_____
_____
_____

Galatians 6:9

Day 4

And let us not be weary in well doing: for in due season we shall reap, if we faint not.

_____

_____

_____

_____

_____

_____

_____

_____

_____

_____

_____

_____

_____

_____

Philippians 1:6

Day 5

Being confident of this very thing, that he which hath begun a good work in you will perform it until the day of Jesus Christ.

_____

_____

_____

_____

_____

_____

_____

_____

_____

_____

_____

_____

_____

Proverbs 3:5-6

Day 6

Trust in the Lord with all thine heart; and lean not unto your own understanding. In all thy ways acknowledge him, and he shall direct thy paths.

_____
_____
_____
_____
_____
_____
_____
_____
_____
_____
_____
_____
_____

Philippians 4:19

Day 7

But my God shall supply all your need according to his riches in glory by Christ Jesus.

_____
_____
_____
_____
_____
_____
_____
_____
_____
_____
_____
_____
_____
_____
_____

John 10:10

"The thief does not come except to steal, and to kill, and to destroy. I have come that they may have life, and that they may have it more abundantly."

Day 8

Proverbs 18:10

Day 9

The name of the Lord is a strong tower,
the righteous run to it and are safe.

_____
_____
_____
_____
_____
_____
_____
_____
_____
_____
_____
_____
_____
_____

II Timothy 1:7

Day 10

For God has not given us a spirit of fear,
but of power and of love and of a sound mind.

_____

_____

_____

_____

_____

_____

_____

_____

_____

_____

_____

_____

_____

Isaiah 54:17

No weapon this is formed against you shall prosper, and every tongue which rises against you in judgment you shall condemn. This is the heritage of the servants of the Lord and their righteousness is of me, says the Lord.

Day 11

Jeremiah 29:11

Day 12

For I know the thoughts that I think towards you, says the Lord, thoughts of peace and not of evil, to give you a future and a hope.

_____

_____

_____

_____

_____

_____

_____

_____

_____

_____

_____

_____

_____

Luke 10:19

"Behold I give you the authority to trample on serpents and scorpions, and over all the power of the enemy, and nothing shall by any means hurt you."

Day 13

_____

_____

_____

_____

_____

_____

_____

_____

_____

_____

_____

_____

_____

_____

Philippians 4:13

Day 14

I can do all things through Christ who strengthens me.

_____

_____

_____

_____

_____

_____

_____

_____

_____

_____

_____

_____

_____

_____

Matthew 11:28

Day 15

"Come unto me, all ye that labour and are heavy laden, and I will give you rest."

_____

_____

_____

_____

_____

_____

_____

_____

_____

_____

_____

_____

_____

Isaiah 41:10

Day 16

Fear not, for I am with you; be not dismayed, for I am your God. I will strengthen you, yes, I will help you, I will uphold you with My righteous right hand.

_____

_____

_____

_____

_____

_____

_____

_____

_____

_____

_____

_____

_____

_____

Mark 9:23

Day 17

Jesus said to him, "If you can believe,
all things are possible to him who believes."

Matthew 5:10

"Blessed are those who are persecuted for righteousness' sake, for theirs is the kingdom of Heaven.

Day 18

John 14:27

Day 19

"Peace I leave with you, My peace I give to you; not as the world gives do I give to you. Let not your heart be troubled, neither let it be afraid."

Psalms 34:19

Day 20

Many are the afflictions of the righteous,
but the Lord delivers him out of them all.

_____

_____

_____

_____

_____

_____

_____

_____

_____

_____

_____

_____

_____

Romans 8:28

And we know all things work together for good to them that love God, to them who are the called according to his purpose.

Day 21

Scripture Translation Cross Reference

Amos 3:3

KJV   Can two walk together, except they be agreed?

NKJV Can two walk together, unless they are agreed?

NIV   Do two walk together unless they have agreed to do so?

I Samuel 15:22

KJV   And Samuel said, Hath the Lord as great delight in burnt offerings and sacrifices, as in obeying the voice of the Lord? Behold, to obey is better than sacrifice, and to hearken than the fat of rams.

NKJV So Samuel said: "Has the Lord as great delight in burnt offerings and sacrifices, as in obeying the voice of the Lord? Behold, to obey is better than sacrifice, and to heed than the fat of rams.

NIV   But Samuel replied: "Does the LORD delight in burnt offerings and sacrifices as much as in obeying the LORD? To obey is better than sacrifice, and to heed is better than the fat of rams.

James 1:17

KJV   Every good gift and every perfect gift is from above, and cometh down from the Father of lights, with whom is no variableness, neither shadow of turning.

NKJV Every good gift and every perfect gift is from above, and comes down from the Father of lights, with whom there is no variation or shadow of turning.

NIV   Every good and perfect gift is from above, coming down from the Father of the heavenly lights, who does not change like shifting shadows.

Isaiah 53:5

KJV But he was wounded for our transgressions, he was bruised for our iniquities: the chastisement of our peace was upon him; and with his stripes we are healed.

NKJV But he was wounded for our transgressions, He was bruised for our iniquities; the chastisement for our peace was upon Him, and by His stripes we are healed.

NIV But he was pierced for our transgressions, he was crushed for our iniquities; the punishment that brought us peace was on him, and by his wounds we are healed.

Luke 4:23

KJV And he said unto them, Ye will surely say unto me this proverb, Physician, heal thyself: whatsoever we have heard done in Capernaum, do also here in they country.

NKJV He said to them, "You will surely say this proverb to Me, 'Physician, heal yourself! Whatever we have heard done in Capernaum, do also here in Your country.'"

NIV Jesus said to them, "Surely you will quote this proverb to me: 'Physician, heal yourself!' And you will tell me, 'Do here in your hometown what we have heard that you did in Capernaum.'"

Matthew 9:29

KJV Then touched he their eyes, saying, According to your faith be it unto you.

NKJV Then He touched their eyes, saying, "According to your faith let it be to you."

NIV Then he touched their eyes and said, "According to your faith let it be done to you";

Matthew 10:33

KJV   But whosoever shall deny me before men, him will I also deny before my Father which is in heaven.

NKJV But whoever denies Me before men, him I will also deny before My Father who is in heaven.

NIV   But whoever disowns me before others, I will disown before my Father in heaven.

II Corinthians 5:17

KJV   Therefore if any man be in Christ, he is a new creature: old things are passed away; behold, all things are become new.

NKJV Therefore, if anyone is in Christ, he is a new creation; old things have passed away; behold, all things have become new.

NIV   Therefore, if anyone is in Christ, the new creation has come: The old has gone, the new is here!

Mark 11:24

KJV   Therefore I say unto you, What things soever ye desire, when ye pray, believe that ye receive them, and ye shall have them.

NKJV Therefore I say to you, whatever things you ask when you pray, believe that you have receive them, and you will have them.

NIV   Therefore I tell you, whatever you ask for in prayer, believe that you have received it, and it will be yours.

Psalms 107:2

KJV   Let the redeemed of the Lord say so, whom he hath redeemed from the hand of the enemy;

NKJV Let the redeemed of the Lord say so, whom He has redeemed from the hand of the enemy,

NIV   Let the redeemed of the LORD tell their story—those he redeemed from the hand of the foe,

Hebrews 8:12

KJV For I will be merciful to their unrighteousness, and their sins and their iniquities will I remember no more.

NKJV For I will be merciful to their unrighteousness, and their sins and their lawless deeds I will remember no more.

NIV For I will forgive their wickedness and will remember their sins no more.

I Peter 2:9-10

KJV But ye are a chosen generation, a royal priesthood, an holy nation, a peculiar people; that ye should shew forth the praises of him who hath called you out of darkness into his marvelous light: Which in time past were not a people, but are now the people of God: which had not obtained mercy, but now have obtained mercy.

NKJV But you are a chosen generation, a royal priesthood, a holy nation, His own special people, that you may proclaim the praises of Him who called you out of darkness into His marvelous light;

NIV But you are a chosen people, a royal priesthood, a holy nation, God's special possession, that you may declare the praises of him who called you out of darkness into his wonderful light. Once you were not a people, but now you are the people of God; once you had not received mercy, but now you have received mercy.

Romans 8:1

KJV There is therefore now no condemnation to them which are in Christ Jesus, who walk not after the flesh, but after the Spirit.

NKJV There is therefore now no condemnation to those who are in Christ Jesus, who do not walk according to the flesh, but according to the Spirit.

NIV Therefore, there is now no condemnation for those who are in Christ Jesus,

Philippians 4:7

KJV And the peace of God, which passeth all understanding, shall keep your hearts and minds through Christ Jesus.

NKJV and the peace of God, which surpasses all understanding, will guard your hearts and minds through Christ Jesus.

NIV And the peace of God, which transcends all understanding, will guard your hearts and your minds in Christ Jesus.

Philippians 4:8

KJV Finally, brethren, whatsoever things are true, whatsoever things are honest, whatsoever things are just, whatsoever things are pure, whatsoever things are lovely, whatsoever things are of good report; if there be any virtue, and if there be any praise, think on these things.

NKJV Finally, brethren, whatever things are true, whatever things are noble, whatever things are just, whatever things are pure, whatever things are lovely, whatever things are of good report, if there is any virtue and if there is anything praiseworthy-meditate on these things.

NIV Finally, brothers and sisters, whatever is true, whatever is noble, whatever is right, whatever is pure, whatever is lovely, whatever is admirable—if anything is excellent or praiseworthy—think about such things.

Proverbs 22:6

KJV Train up a child in the way he should go: and when he is old, he will not depart from it.

NKJV Train up a child in the way he should go, and when he is old he will not depart from it.

NIV Start children off on the way they should go, and even when they are old they will not turn from it.

Isaiah 30:18

KJV   And therefore will the Lord wait, that he may be gracious unto you, and therefore will he be exalted, that he may have mercy upon you: for the Lord is a God of judgment: blessed are all they that wait for him.

NKJV Therefore the Lord will wait, that He may be gracious to you; and therefore He will be exalted, that He may have mercy on you.

NIV   Yet the LORD longs to be gracious to you; therefore he will rise up to show you compassion. For the LORD is a God of justice. Blessed are all who wait for him!

Mark 11:22

KJV   And Jesus answering saith unto them, Have faith in God.

NKJV So Jesus answered and said to them, "Have faith in God."

NIV   "Have faith in God," Jesus answered.

Hebrews 11:1

KJV   Now faith is the substance of things hoped for, the evidence of things not seen.

NKJV Now faith is the substance of things hoped for, the evidence of things not seen.

NIV   Now faith is confidence in what we hope for and assurance about what we do not see.

John 5:24

KJV   Verily, verily, I say unto you, He that heareth my word, and believeth on him that   sent me, hath everlasting life, and shall not come into condemnation; but is passed from death unto life.

NKJV Most assuredly, I say to you, he who hears My word and believes in Him who sent Me has everlasting life, and shall not come into judgment, but has passed from death into life.

NIV   "Very truly I tell you, whoever hears my word and believes him who sent me has eternal life and will not be judged but has crossed over from death to life.

Proverbs 4:7

KJV   Wisdom is the principal thing; therefore get wisdom: and with all thy getting get understanding.

NKJV Wisdom is the principal thing; therefore get wisdom. And in all your getting, get understanding.

NIV   The beginning of wisdom is this: Get wisdom. Though it cost all you have, get understanding.

Romans 8:1

KJV   There is therefore now no condemnation to them which are in Christ Jesus, who walk not after the flesh, but after the Spirit.

NKJV There is therefore now no condemnation to those who are in Christ Jesus, who do not walk according to the flesh, but according to the Spirit.

NIV   Therefore, there is now no condemnation for those who are in Christ Jesus,

Romans 8:28

KJV   And we know that all things work together for good to them that love God, to them who are the called according to his purpose.

NKJV And we know that all things work together for good to those who love God, to those who are the called according to His purpose.

NIV   And we know that in all things God works for the good of those who love him, who have been called according to his purpose.

Isaiah 55:9

KJV   For as the heavens are higher than the earth, so are my ways higher than your ways, and my thoughts than your thoughts

NKJV For as the heavens are higher than the earth, so are My ways higher than your ways, and My thoughts than your thoughts.

NIV   "As the heavens are higher than the earth, so are my ways higher than your ways and my thoughts than your thoughts.

Psalms 121:1-2

KJV   I will lift up mine eyes unto the hills, from whence cometh my help. My help cometh from the Lord, which made heaven and earth.

NKJV I will lift up my eyes to the hills-from whence comes my help? My help comes from the Lord, who made heaven and earth.

NIV   I lift up my eyes to the mountains— where does my help come from? My help comes from the LORD, the Maker of heaven and earth.

Philippians 4:13

KJV   I can do all things through Christ which strengtheneth me.

NKJV I can do all things through Christ who strengthens me.

NIV   I can do all this through him who gives me strength.

Colossians 3:1-2

KJV   If ye then be risen with Christ, seek those things which are above, where Christ sitteth on the right hand of God. Set your affection on things above, not on things of the earth.

NKJV If then you were raised with Christ, seek those things which are above, where Christ is, sitting at the right hand of God. Set your mind on things above, not on things on the earth.

NIV   Since, then, you have been raised with Christ, set your hearts on things above, where Christ is, seated at the right hand of God. 2 Set your minds on things above, not on earthly things.

Revelations 3:15-16

KJV   I know thy works, that thou art neither cold nor hot: I would thou wert cold or hot. So then because thou art lukewarm, and neither cold nor hot, I will spue thee out of my mouth.

NKJV I know your works, that you are neither cold nor hot, I could wish you were cold or hot. So then, because you are lukewarm, and neither cold nor hot, I will vomit you out of My mouth.

NIV   I know your deeds, that you are neither cold nor hot. I wish you were either one or the other! So, because you are lukewarm—neither hot nor cold—I am about to spit you out of my mouth.

Psalms 118:8

KJV   It is better to trust in the Lord than to put confidence in man.

NKJV It is better to trust in the Lord than to put confidence in man.

NIV   It is better to take refuge in the LORD than to trust in humans.

Romans 10:17

KJV So then faith cometh by hearing, and hearing by the word of God.

NKJV So then faith comes by hearing, and hearing by the word of God.

NIV Consequently, faith comes from hearing the message, and the message is heard through the word about Christ.

Psalms 27:14

KJV Wait on the Lord: be of good courage, and he shall strengthen thine heart: wait, I say, on the Lord.

NKJV Wait on the Lord; be of good courage, and He shall strengthen your heart; wait, I say, on the Lord!

NIV Wait for the LORD; be strong and take heart and wait for the LORD.

Isaiah 26:3

KJV Thou wilt keep him in perfect peace, whose mind is stayed on thee: because he trusteth in thee.

NKJV You will keep him in perfect peace, whose mind is stayed on You, because he trusts in You.

NIV You will keep in perfect peace those whose minds are steadfast, because they trust in you.

II Corinthians 12:9

KJV And he said unto me, My grace is sufficient for thee: for my strength is made perfect in weakness. Most gladly therefore will I rather glory in my infirmities, that the power of Christ may rest upon me.

NKJV And He said to me, "My grace is sufficient for you, for My strength is made perfect in weakness."

NIV But he said to me, "My grace is sufficient for you, for my power is made perfect in weakness." Therefore I will boast all the more gladly about my weaknesses, so that Christ's power may rest on me.

Galatians 6:9

KJV   And let us not be weary in well doing: for in due season we shall reap, if we faint not.

NKJV And let us not grow weary while doing good, for in due season we shall reap if we do not lose heart.

NIV   Let us not become weary in doing good, for at the proper time we will reap a harvest if we do not give up.

Philippians 1:6

KJV   Being confident of this very thing, that he which hath begun a good work in you will perform it until the day of Jesus Christ:

NKJV being confident of this very thing, that He who has begun a good work in you will complete it until the day of Jesus Christ;

NIV   being confident of this, that he who began a good work in you will carry it on to completion until the day of Christ Jesus.

Proverbs 3:5-6

KJV   Trust in the Lord with all thine heart; and lean not unto thine own understanding. In all thy ways acknowledge him, and he shall direct thy paths.

NKJV Trust in the Lord with all your heart, and lean not on your own understanding; in all your ways acknowledge Him, and He shall direct your paths.

NIV   Trust in the LORD with all your heart and lean not on your own understanding; in all your ways submit to him, and he will make your paths straight.

Philippians 4:19

KJV   But my God shall supply all your need according to his riches in glory by Christ Jesus.

NKJV   And my God shall supply all your need according to His riches in glory by Christ Jesus.

NIV   And my God will meet all your needs according to the riches of his glory in Christ Jesus.

John 10:10

KJV   The thief cometh not, but for to steal, and to kill, and to destroy: I am come that they might have life, and that they might have it more abundantly.

NKJV   The thief does not come except to steal, and to kill, and to destroy. I have come that they may have life, and that they may have it more abundantly.

NIV   The thief comes only to steal and kill and destroy; I have come that they may have life, and have it to the full.

Proverbs 18:10

KJV   The name of the Lord is a strong tower: the righteous runneth into it, and is safe.

NKJV   The name of the Lord is a strong tower; the righteous run to it and are safe.

NIV   The name of the LORD is a fortified tower; the righteous run to it and are safe.

II Timothy 1:7

KJV   For God hath not given us the spirit of fear; but of power, and of love, and of a sound mind.

NKJV   For God has not given us a spirit of fear, but of power and of love and of a sound mind.

NIV   For the Spirit God gave us does not make us timid, but gives us power, love and self-discipline.

Isaiah 54:17

KJV   No weapon that is formed against thee shall prosper; and every tongue that shall rise against thee in judgment thou shalt condemn. This is the heritage of the servants of the Lord, and their righteousness is of me, saith the Lord.

NKJV No weapon formed against you shall prosper, and every tongue which rises against you in judgment you shall condemn. This is the heritage of the servants of the Lord, and their righteousness is from Me, says the Lord

NIV   no weapon forged against you will prevail, and you will refute every tongue that accuses you. This is the heritage of the servants of the LORD, and this is their vindication from me," declares the LORD.

Jeremiah 29:11

KJV   For I know the thoughts that I think toward you, saith the Lord, thoughts of peace, and not of evil, to give you an expected end.

NKJV For I know the thoughts that I think toward you, says the Lord, thoughts of peace and not of evil, to give you a future and a hope.

NIV   For I know the plans I have for you," declares the LORD, "plans to prosper you and not to harm you, plans to give you hope and a future.

Luke 10:19

KJV   Behold, I give unto you power to tread on serpents and scorpions, and over all the power of the enemy:and nothing shall by any means hurt you.

NKJV Behold, I give you the authority to trample on serpents and scorpions, and over all the power of the enemy, and nothing shall by any means hurt you.

NIV   I have given you authority to trample on snakes and scorpions and to overcome all the power of the enemy; nothing will harm you.

Philippians 4:13

KJV   I can do all things through Christ which strengtheneth me.

NKJV I can do all things through Christ who strengthens me.

NIV   I can do all this through him who gives me strength.

Matthew 11:28

KJV   Come unto me, all ye that labour and are heavy laden, and I will give you rest.

NKJV Come to Me, all you who labor and are heavy laden, and I will give you rest.

NIV   "Come to me, all you who are weary and burdened, and I will give you rest.

Isaiah 41:10

KJV   Fear thou not; for I am with thee: be not dismayed; for I am thy God: I will strengthen thee; yea, I will help thee; yea, I will uphold thee with the right hand of my righteousness.

NKJV Fear not, for I am with you; be not dismayed, for I am your God. I will strengthen you, yes, I will help you, I will uphold you with My righteous right hand.

NIV   So do not fear, for I am with you; do not be dismayed, for I am your God. I will strengthen you and help you; I will uphold you with my righteous right hand.

Mark 9:23

KJV   Jesus said unto him, If thou canst believe, all things are possible to him that believeth.

NKJV Jesus said to him, "If you can believe, all things are possible to him who believes."

NIV   "'If you can'?" said Jesus. "Everything is possible for one who believes."

Matthew 5:10

KJV   Blessed are they which are persecuted for righteousness' sake: for their's is the kingdom of heaven.

NKJV Blessed are those who are persecuted for righteousness' sake, for theirs is the kingdom of heaven.

NIV   Blessed are those who are persecuted because of righteousness, for theirs is the k   ingdom of heaven.

John 14:27

KJV   Peace I leave with you, my peace I give unto you: not as the world giveth, give I unto you. Let not your heart be troubled, neither let it be afraid.

NKJV Peace I leave with you, My peace I give to you; not as the world gives do I give to you. Let not your heart be troubled, neither let it be afraid.

NIV   Peace I leave with you; my peace I give you. I do not give to you as the world gives. Do not let your hearts be troubled and do not be afraid.

Psalms 34:19

KJV   Many are the afflictions of the righteous: but the Lord delivereth him out of them all.

NKJV Many are the afflictions of the righteous, but the Lord delivers him out of them all.

NIV   The righteous person may have many troubles, but the LORD delivers him from them all;

Romans 8:28

KJV   And we know that all things work together for good to them that love God, to them who are the called according to his purpose.

NKJV And we know that all things work together for good to those who love God, to those who are the called according to His purpose.

NIV   And we know that in all things God works for the good of those who love him, who have been called according to his purpose.

Acknowledgements

There is only one acknowledgement that needs to be made, and that is to God. It is He alone that is responsible for this book becoming a reality. He put a desire in my heart years ago to write. He blessed me with spiritual growth as a result of the events of 2013. He encouraged me immediately thereafter to put my thoughts on paper. He has assured me that there is a message within that will serve as encouragement for others.

When I encountered moments of uncertainty during the writing and publishing process, He provided me with clarity and direction. When I cried while recounting some of the most painful times of my life, He wiped me tears and wrapped His ever-loving arms around me to remind me that it's over and I survived.

But by the grace of God
I am what I am,
and His grace toward me did not prove vain;
but I labored even more than all of them,
yet not I,
but the grace of God with me.
I Corinthians 15:10

About The Author

Although she has previously published poems and articles, Shawn-Ta Sterns Wilson makes her book publishing debut with Survival by Faith. After a series of life-changing events, Shawn-Ta felt a spiritual calling to document her journey. The surreal experiences she vividly details will enlighten and encourage you in your faith walk. Those experiences have altered the course of her life forever, in very positive ways. Each one served to strengthen and better equip her for life.

Born in Connecticut and raised in Virginia, Shawn-Ta now lives in Florida. Shawn-Ta is a Certified Meeting Professional (CMP) and her career in the convention industry has spanned more than twenty-five years. In that time she has successfully managed events ranging in size from ten to 20,000 people. Her expertise was acknowledged when she received the nationally awarded Convention Services Manager of the Year award.

Shawn-Ta often says she is an average, ordinary person which makes her story all the more relatable to readers. Her writing style inspires, encourages, and gives hope.

Shawn-Ta continues to share her testimony of faith with others by speaking with groups and at conferences.

80633567R00120

Made in the USA
Columbia, SC
09 November 2017